To Jerry + Maureen,
You are right - books
are fun. In this case it was
my sisters who did the writing.
Meg + Steve

SO WE BECAME FARMERS

SO WE BECAME FARMERS

A MEMOIR

Steve Lanphear and Meg Lanphear

SO WE BECAME FARMERS
Steve Lanphear and Meg Lanphear

Published by
The Cheshire Press
an imprint of The Cheshire Group
Andover, MA 01810
www.cheshirepress.com

Copyright © 2018 by Steve and Meg Lanphear
ISBN: 978-0-9995092-6-5
Library of Congress Control Number: 20189505882

Printed in the United States of America

Cover design by Nancy Parsons
Back cover photographs:
Nancy Parsons: Fjords/apple orchard
Bob Buehler: Hen and goat
Myndi Bogdanovich: Family/Steve and Meg:

Lanphear, Steve
Lanphear, Meg

To our family,

To the memory of our parents,

And remembering Aunt Mary

who always worried about the farmers

SO WE BECAME FARMERS

SO WE BECAME FARMERS

My long two-pointed ladder's sticking through a tree
Toward heaven still,
And there's a barrel that I didn't fill
Beside it, and there may be two or three
Apples I didn't pick upon some bough.
But I am done with apple picking now.

After Apple Picking
Robert Frost

SO WE BECAME FARMERS

TABLE OF CONTENTS

SO WE BECAME FARMERS

INTRODUCTION

At a time when the number of farms in America was dwindling at alarming rates, we enrolled our small agricultural operation in the USDA Farm Service Agency database and prepared to write "farmers" on the occupation line of the IRS forms. And so, optimistically, with one small-holding, we bucked the trend. We became farmers.

Old farmers, to be sure. But that was to our advantage. We already looked like farmers, and years earlier, we found that splitting wood and raising a couple of pigs was more appealing than shopping trips through Nordstrom's. So when most of our friends were planning retirements filled with cruises and golf games, we turned to farming fulltime.

Why did we think we could become farmers? And why did we think we'd be successful? The questions are good ones, especially considering what Meg's mother had to say about it. Maggie's opinions—uninvited and often uninformed—were daily rations. About farming, she said: "You can't just *be* a farmer—you have to be born into it."

We hadn't been. Born into it, that is. We'd both been born in Ohio not far from Cleveland.

But in this case, we took Maggie's point and, without the advantage of birth, we set about learning how to become farmers.

The first thing we did was ask around. Luckily, we live in Belchertown, Massachusetts, at the southern tip of the Quabbin Reservoir and deep in the Pioneer Valley. In this ancient rift, between the Berkshire Mountains and the Eastern Massachusetts hills, the retreating arm of the sea during the Triassic era, left unusually fertile soil that supports a number of highly productive farms. Belchertown itself is a blend of small town and rural life that has started to look more suburban since developers began setting out housing plats on the acres where farmers once set out young cabbages and planted fruit trees.

Still, there are farms, large and small ones, in and around Belchertown and plenty of old-time farmers, so there was no lack of talent to tap for advice. We hung our sign for Sentinel Farm and hoped the Valley would support one more farm.

Steve Lanphear
Meg Lanphear

THE BACK STORY

Steve

We got started gradually—you know, the way you can't always tell when something is beginning—but then one day you turn around and notice where you are, and maybe you look back down a long road and see how far you've come. It happened slowly, this business of becoming farmers. But times were different then. When we started, times were different.

Meg

We were living on Bay Road in Belchertown. It was around 1972, I guess, and Steve and I were still students at UMass Amherst. We were studying and making a little money on the side, although very little. I was working my way toward a Masters degree in physical therapy and was getting a small stipend from teaching an anatomy class, and Steve was plowing snow and working freelance landscape projects. We'd lived in rentals in Amherst for two years and we'd moved seven times. We were tired of it. We wanted our own place—a place we wouldn't have to leave unless we wanted to. And we found that place in the town next door—Belchertown. We borrowed some money from our families and scraped up the rest and bought the house for $14,000.

If you want to know what the house looked like, imagine a shoebox. The house wasn't much bigger than a shoebox either. If you put a piece of cardboard lengthwise in that box, you'd see the layout. On one side of this divider were a kitchen and the front room; on the other side were three bedrooms and a bathroom. With a little girl in each room, plus the main bedroom, which was only slightly larger than the double bed in it, we were full up. Still the house sat on a square acre that supported a vegetable garden, and we'd added a screened porch that eased some of the congestion inside the house.

I didn't mind the house on Bay Road. The only dark side as far as I could see was the rumor that Bay Road was going to be rerouted and a housing development was going in. Malvina Reynolds's song about little boxes on a hillside was popular, and I didn't like the thought of ticky-tacky houses growing up around me. Steve, I think, had grander thoughts.

Steve

I don't remember when I first saw the abandoned house on Cottage Street. I think I became aware of it gradually so I don't exactly remember when I actually decided it was a project we could—or should—take on. I do remember that I was doing some volunteer work in Belchertown and was getting to know some local people. I asked around and found out that the house belonged to Eleanor Schmidt.

Now Eleanor was a force in Belchertown. She was a former selectwoman and she was among the last of an old family that had been displaced when the valley was flooded to create the Quabbin Reservoir. Also, she was very interested in history.

Well, I got in touch with Eleanor, said that my wife and I were interested in buying the house, and there began a negotiation that took a year or more.

So Meg and I went over to meet Eleanor Schmidt and her husband Eddie. He was a big guy with very strong opinions which he expressed loudly, and those opinions were usually the exact opposite of Eleanor's, but the house belonged to her so what she said usually trumped what Eddie had to say. That didn't stop him from expressing his views though, and good old Eleanor, who must have had selective deafness, went right on ignoring them and doing what she wanted. In her years on the selectman's board, she'd made a point of keeping a direct line into the town's business. Not much got past her, and when an interesting historical property came on the market, Eleanor was right there with her checkbook open. That's how she'd acquired the place on Cottage Street. The Schmidts never lived there. They just paid the taxes and waited for whatever. "Whatever" hadn't amounted to anything in thirteen years. Or it hadn't until Meg and I came along.

A house needs to be lived in. If it isn't occupied, it starts sagging at the knees and losing its teeth and thirteen years of vacancy had taken its toll.

Meg

My mother was visiting when we were invited to see the Schmidt's house, so of course she went along with us. Like Eleanor and Eddie, she had opinions too—lots of them. But she had the sense to keep most of them to herself...well, until later when she had plenty to say. Her opinions ran along the lines of "What were you thinking?"... "How do you ever suppose...?" "How could you raise children in a place like that...?"

Eleanor Schmidt didn't like me. Wouldn't even look at me.

She only talked to Steve. I don't know, maybe it was a gender thing, but that's the way it was. Eddie Schmidt, on the other hand, liked my mother, and she thought he was wonderful, because they agreed on almost everything, I suppose.

Anyhow, the five of us went over to Cottage Street and began going through the house. Eleanor led the way and Steve kept up with her. We started in the cellar, and there wasn't much to that since it was just a big room with a dirt floor. Then we climbed a ladder to reach the main floor. Eleanor went first, talking back over her shoulder to Steve who was climbing up behind her. I followed Steve, and then came my mother with Eddie climbing inappropriately close to her backside.

So there was Eleanor, pointing out all the charms and advantages of the place, and Steve was taking it all in and nodding encouragingly and asking a million questions and at the back of the group, Eddie was voicing his opinions, and not quietly either. He had always been hoping for arson, he said. Praying someone would come in and torch the place.

"Look here," he said to my mother, opening a closet door. "See that char? Some kids actually tried to burn the place down. Too bad they didn't succeed."

"Oh my," said my mother.

That's all she said the whole time. "Oh my. Oh *my*!"

Eleanor ignored him.

Well, Steve eventually got around to asking the price of the house and that subject kept them occupied for the rest of the afternoon and for the better part of the year afterward. Eleanor was reluctant to sell. Kept talking about the historical value of the place. Steve was persistent however, and when he wants to, he can do quite a bit of sweet-talking. He's good at that.

Steve

Yes, it did take more than a year to settle our negotiation, but Eleanor and I kept at it. In the end, she and I were down to gnarling over one strip of land at the edge of the property that she wanted to keep for some reason. But I told her no. No, that strip was what we liked about the place. We wanted the wood lot and if she insisted on breaking that away, the deal was off. By that time, Eleanor Schmidt wasn't getting any younger and she was probably imagining how nice our money was going to look in her bank account, so she reluctantly let that strip of land go.

Twelve acres of land went with the house as well as two outbuildings. One was a small barn built into a hill and it was in worse condition than the house. But the other building had been the office and printing establishment of *The Belchertown Sentinel,* the town's newspaper, and it was in pretty good shape. A fellow named Lewis Blackmer had been the editor. He started the paper in 1915, and he lived in the house before Eleanor Schmidt bought it. He ran the newspaper out of the building in back of the house, and it was still stuffed with Blackmer's clobber—printing presses and racks and even the papers on the editor's desk. As part of the sales' deal, we agreed to Eleanor's demand that the contents of the place would be donated to The Stone House Museum in the town center. We were happy to do that, because I couldn't imagine where else we'd get rid of the crap. It was an awful chore to clean out the place though, to dismantle and unload all the stuff and get it over to the museum, but we managed it.

Now while we were waiting for Eleanor to come to a sales settlement, we started doing some demolition on the house. This was okay with the Schmidts, and none of us had the sense to know that it could be a legally dangerous undertaking, so Meg and I got some hammers swinging and worked nights after work, even though the house wasn't yet ours. You couldn't do that today with all the litigation. As I said, the times were different.

Meg

I'm going to describe what our property looked like so you can get "the lay of the land" or have a sort of map so you can picture what we're talking about.

Cottage Street leaves the east side of Belchertown Common and runs downhill past Skinners's house and their apple orchard and pasture; then it reaches the kitchen door of Eleanor's house (that used to be Blackmer's house and the *Belchertown Sentinel* and eventually became our house). There the street bangs a ninety-degree turn and runs downhill again, beside the long front property all the way to East Walnut Street.

Eventually we painted the house yellow (and painted it again and again over the years) and we started calling it the Yellow House, but when we moved in, it was unpainted and gray. You know how people are always saying a house has good bones? Well, this house did, even though some of them were fragile like the bones of an old lady with osteoporosis, except, unlike an old lady's bones, we could see how these bones could be restored. Or at least that's what Steve said.

You could see where it could be a good-looking house, though—a square farmhouse with a central front door. If you turned right, you walked into a large square sitting room with plenty of morning sun. If you went left, you were in the parlor where eventually there was a woodstove. Behind these rooms were a large country kitchen, a dining room and a small bedroom as well as an annex behind the kitchen that could be used for a pantry and everything else. And cold! That house had the worst time holding heat. But we got used to it.

The house needed work. Well, that understates it—it was

uninhabitable. We couldn't wait to move in.

Steve

It didn't take us long to realize that whacking away with our hammers at night wasn't going to turn that house into a home—not for years and years. So Meg and I discussed it and came up with a plan.

Meg would continue working, taking a job in the physical therapy department at the Belchertown State School, and she would be the family breadwinner. I would resign my position on the planning board of the City of Holyoke and would handle the construction and at the same time would keep an eye on the kids.

Now if I were speaking to you in person—face to face— right here I would be holding my sides laughing at my ignorant innocence.

"Keep an eye on the kids."

Yeah. Right.

Abby was four-years-old and Molly was two. They required more—much more—than an eye being kept on them. Much of what they required involved running on the part of the person keeping the eye. Moreover, I felt responsible for preparing the family meals and in preparation for that, I'd bought myself a wok so I could stir up quick, healthful dinners comprised of plenty of fresh vegetables.

Do you have any idea how long it takes a man, who is renovating a house and keeping an eye on two pre-schoolers, to gather and chop enough vegetables for a nourishing stir-fry? A man who has to do this day after day? Instead of sawing wood to repair joists, I stopped what I was doing every afternoon at three to start julienning carrots and scallions and bok choy.

While I was working away on the house, I realized at some

point, that if the Print House were habitable, we could rent it and get a bit of additional income. So putting the Yellow House construction on temporary hold, I transferred my time and attention to the Print House.

Meanwhile, inside the Yellow House, we continued to live in the state of dust and confusion that construction always causes.

Meg

The plan sounded pretty good when we thought it up, but after a year or two, it was beginning to get me. For one thing—just one thing—there was a hole in the ceiling of our bedroom. We had covered it temporarily with a big piece of fabric, but the mice who lived in the attic couldn't seem to distinguish between what was their territory and what was ours. The night a mouse ran directly across our bed, running over both of us as it went, was enough.

I whined about it all to the girls' nursery school teacher who had been through a similar construction situation several years before. She consoled me.

"It will end," she said. "It will be worth it. And you will survive."

Some days I doubted it but there were other times when I could see the funny side.

Steve had ripped out the wall between the bathroom and the kitchen and had only gotten as far as constructing a half wall between the rooms. Above the waist, a line of studs suggested that a whole wall would be there...someday.

The minister came to call one day, bringing his wife. She asked to use the powder room. Embarrassed, we pointed out our semi-private accommodation. She was unflappable, this woman. Amazing. She sailed into the bathroom, sat down on the toilet, and speaking through the studs, simply continued the story she'd started telling in the kitchen. And in the kitchen we just sat there in astonishment and listened to everything. And I mean everything. We've never got over it.

Steve

When we'd gotten the Print House to the place where it was fit to rent, we also got Andrea. She was our tenant. The rent check was welcome, but as I said, there in the middle of it all was Andrea. She was a social worker and therefore an expert on just about everything.

About this time it seemed a good idea to raise a few pigs. I suppose this is the first documented instance of our farming, but I have to tell you that raising a couple of pigs does not qualify anyone as a farmer.

While this plan was still just a talking point, Bruce Jacques, our neighbor down the road, heard about it and invited himself in.

"Oh sure," he said convincingly, "raising a pig is almost no trouble at all. You just feed them garbage and compost, clean out the pen once in a while, and come Fall you slaughter them and there's meat for the winter. I even know a guy who'll do the slaughtering."

Bruce was persuasive. Meg and I looked at each other. Meat for the winter. Sounded good. And how hard can it be?

Apparently, Bruce was such a good salesman that he persuaded himself. He explained that he knew someone who worked at the Hood factory over in Agawam, and he volunteered to bring lots of expired cottage cheese to feed the pigs if we would let him in on the deal.

So we got two pigs, one for Bruce and one for us, and we built a pen. We built it a little closer to the house than we should have but chalk it up a farming learning experience. All summer we fed the pigs compost and plenty of out-of-code

Hood cottage cheese.

In the fall I asked Bruce again about his friend.

"Frank, yeah."

Warning me that the guy could be a little rough and could only work on days when he hadn't been drinking heavily the night before, Bruce agreed to line up an appointment.

It was an event. Meg's mother was again visiting us and was supervising a highly curious and inquisitive Abby and Molly. Andrea was present also, and prepared to explain the whole process to the by-standers, although I had to wonder how much experience with pig butchering a Jewish girl from New York City had.

The pigs were shot and hung by ropes looped around the branch of a huge old ash tree beside the barn. With a cigarette hanging from his lip and the scent of last-night's binge in the air, Frank slit the first pig.

Andrea, who had been narrating the event for the benefit of Abby and Molly, used the moment to illustrate a lesson in health.

"See," she told the little girls, "those are the pig's lungs. See how nice and pink they are? That's because the pig didn't *smoke*."

She glanced meaningfully at the slaughterer.

"If the pig had *smoked*," she continued, "its lungs would be all filthy and *gray*!"

Frank gave Andrea a look of disgust and waggled the cigarette on his lip.

The process continued. Eventually Frank began pulling out the intestines and neighboring parts. Andrea was puzzled.

"What are those?" she wanted to know.

Frank didn't like Andrea.

"Those?" he repeated, speaking around his cigarette. "If you don't know what those are by now, sweetheart, you'll never know."

The carcasses went off to a butcher in Ware and the meat that was going to sustain us for the winter eventually came back. It wasn't very good.

"It was probably all that rotten cottage cheese," Meg remarked.

"Whatever happened to Andrea?" I wondered once.

"Andrea?" Meg said. "She went to Cleveland."

BUYING THE ORCHARD

Meg

It was around 1984 or '85. I was working as a physical therapist for the Holyoke School system, The administration informed me that I and another person were going to coordinate and lead a program in neurodevelopment treatment—not something I was prepared to do. Then the other person disappeared—vanished or something. I never knew quite where or why, but it didn't matter. What mattered was that I was in charge of setting up the program and providing children to be treated by other therapists from around the country. It was time-consuming and stressful, and I was at my wit's end. And while I was trying to get my head around all this, Steve came up with the Skinner house deal. And he wanted my opinions.

"Do what you want," I said. "I can't be bothered."

"And *you're* the person who's going to teach neuro-development?" he said.

So he went ahead and did what he wanted, and when the

neurodevelopment treatment program finally ended and I came up for air, I found out that we owned another house in addition to the two houses that we already had.

If we stood in the kitchen door of the Yellow House and looked west up Cottage Street past the hill pasture, we could see our new house—formerly our next door neighbors' house—the Skinners' house. It was a white Greek Revival place, but at some point, someone had added a wrap-around front porch. The porch muddled the Greek Revival geometry but for convenience, it was welcome.

From our lower viewing point down the hill, the Skinner House looked dignified and prosperous. There was a big red barn just behind it and beyond that, neat as rows of pipers in a Highland regiment, trees in an apple orchard marched back, probably eight acres to a stone wall.

Arlan Skinner was the president of a local bank, and he ran a cash-crop apple business as a profitable hobby. He employed a professional nurseryman named Sam White to take the orchard through winter, spring and summer, and in the fall, Sam brought in pickers from Jamaica who moved into the the orchard, filling wooden crates and loading them onto trucks that bumped them off to various local markets. And Arlan, good banker that he was, tucked the profits away in a savings account.

Steve

I'd had my eye on the Skinners' place for some time. I don't know, I just thought that running a small orchard would somehow feel just right. Trees, after all, are in my background. For two years, I studied them at the Stockbridge School of Agriculture, and my dad and uncle ran Forest City Tree Protection Co. and Nursery in Cleveland—a business that my grandfather founded. A huge outfit dealing in large-scale trees.

I'm not sure how aware I was of it, but I used to drive by Skinners' every day and I'd look at the orchard with something like lust, imagining what I'd do if it were mine—imagining how I'd make that orchard even better.

So one day I said to Arlan Skinner, "If you ever decide to sell, I'd like the first right of refusal."

"Oh," he said, surprised, "Oh, well, yes. That sounds fine."

So it was my turn to be surprised when I started up the hill one morning on my way to work and spotted a for sale sign in front of the house.

I turned around right in Arlan's driveway and drove home. I grabbed the kitchen phone and called him up.

"Arlan," I said, "I thought you were going to give me first right of refusal if you decided to sell your house."

"Oh," he said. "Well. I guess maybe that's so. Do you want to buy it?"

"Yes!" I said, "I do! How much are you asking?"

So Arlan named a figure and I said, "That sounds fine."

I wasn't going to quibble about price at that point. But I immediately called up Neil McCann at Ludlow Savings Bank and told him what I wanted to do and asked if he thought I could do it.

"I expect you can," he said. He asked me a couple of questions, and we cut the deal right then over the phone.

Well, as I said, it was a different time.

Meg

I guess we were landlords before we were farmers. The girls were growing up but the four of us couldn't live in three houses at one time, so we continued to rent the Print House after Andrea moved to Cleveland, and we went looking for tenants for the Orchard House.

We didn't live in the Orchard House at first, but we

certainly lived on the land. Arlan Skinner relied heavily on his orchard manager who moonlighted from his job at Atkins Orchard—a big orchard and farm stand on the other side of Belchertown not far from our old house on Bay Road. Sam did some spraying in our orchard, and he did some marginal pruning. Steve said that Sam didn't much like to prune and didn't give it proper attention since he did enough of that during his day job. But in the fall, Sam brought over the Jamaicans who had come north to work at Atkins. They'd arrive toward the end of the day and swarm through the orchard, picking and laughing and tossing the apple boxes around as if they were nothing more than matchboxes. We paid Sam a little bit for his work, and we paid the Jamaicans in cases of beer.

Apart from the Jamaicans, Sam's only employee was my mother. And she didn't get any payment—not even beer.

She sorted apples and polished them and stacked them in the apple boxes, which were too heavy for her to lift, but she stuck to her work and took it seriously. I don't think Sam knew what to make of her and one day he looked at her, shook his head and said, "*My* mother plays cards."

That made her mad.

Sam took some of the apples over to Atkins' farm stand, but it was up to my mother and me to sell as much of the crop as we could. Apart from what we sold wholesale to Atkins, we had a customer down in Springfield. We'd drive down to an Italian vegetable stand. Antonio's Market. We sold whatever we hauled for eight dollars a box. A forty-pound box for eight dollars! Imagine. And we hauled the boxes and unloaded them ourselves. My eighty-year-old mother and I, and while we worked, the people at Antonio's just stood around and watched.

Steve

Now about this time—or maybe it was a while before—Meg

and I began to realize that what we were doing was actual farming. We had property. We had a crop. And once in a while, we'd even had farm hands. We still had one, if you counted Meg's mother. We started referring to our holding as Sentinel Farm. The name came easily. So we had a sign made, adding Sentinel Farm to the mythological-looking animal bust used by the *Belchertown Sentinel*.

Our arrangement with Sam went on for a few years but with diminishing returns. Our orchard really wasn't worth Sam's time and one day he left and we were on our own. He left his sprayer though. A real antique that I used for a while, but it was peppered with pinhole leaks and using it became a hazmat issue. That's probably why Sam left it.

After Sam left, the orchard sort of limped along. It was unproductive for a while. And I was starting to realize there was no way I could work full time and handle the orchard too. It was just crazy.

Meg

Well, the orchard wasn't productive but Steve and I had other income since we were still working at our jobs.

For years, I had been trying to convince my mother to move from Ohio to Belchertown so we could keep an eye on her, and finally, the year she turned eighty, she agreed. We gave her a choice of living arrangements—the Print House or Skinner's. Well, she chose the Orchard House. Her reasoning was sort of hard to follow. It involved placing her forearm parallel to the ground and moving it up and down like it was on a jack. The Print House was "down" she claimed and she felt more comfortable on the higher ground of the orchard.

Well, that was fine.

Then a few years later we persuaded Mildred, Steve's mother, to move up from Ohio too. She didn't get a choice of houses though. She got the Print House by default. That was okay because she didn't seem to have Maggie's geological biases.

So now we each had a mother-in-law living quite close so we had the benefit of their opinions. Which were many and were freely and frequently given.

A NEW ERA

Steve

It was 2001. Meg's mother had died the year before and my mother had experienced some kind of medical event, something that old timers might call "a spell." Anyway, she moved up to Vermont to live with my sister Beth, so in a matter of a few months we lost our mothers and our tenants. But in 2001, we launched a bold plan that seemed to repeat a pattern set years before. I decided to retire. Simply go home and tend full time to business there.

As it turned out, I didn't actually retire. I just took up a new occupation that was easily more trouble and time consuming than city planning or insurance. But if we were going to have a successful orchard—the orchard I'd always known was possible when I drove past it during Skinners' time—I knew I'd have to give it my full attention, full time. I couldn't do that while working an eight-to five job. So as before, our plan was for Meg to keep working and bringing in the cash until the orchard started contributing meaningfully.

Meanwhile I would restore and revive the orchard that was the main component of our farm.

Well, Meg and I sat down and took an inventory of where we'd come and what we had.

We owned quite a bit of land. Ever since buying the Yellow House, we'd been picking up a few acres here and there in the woodlot and in the back of the orchard, and our original twelve acres eventually added up to twenty-six acres

Eventually we sold off some of the land as "estate" lots, keeping one lot adjacent to the orchard for "whatever." I guess we'd learned something from Eleanot Schmidt after all.

Meg and I put a for sale sign on the Yellow House and with a few strokes of a pen, we unburdened ourselves of the Yellow House and the Print House. Then we moved up the hill and into Skinners' old house—Orchard House—where Meg's mother had lived for more than a decade. For a number of years we'd kept a horse or two in the old barn beside the Yellow House, and now these animals moved up the hill too and were stabled in the cellar of the big red barn.

We celebrated by upgrading our logo to feature a silhouetted horse and buggy. "Sentinel Farm" it said. We were in a new era.

Meg

I was working at American International College in Springfield when the "new era" began. AIC had started a physical therapy program and as their clinical coordinator, I was finding intern positions for the school's physical therapy students, and I was traveling all over the country to check on these students once they were placed. It was fun up to a point. I had an expense account. I liked that. But eventually I got tired of airports and suitcases and making reservations—I even got sort of tired of the students—so I accepted a quieter position with the school system up in Greenfield. The commute was easier. In good weather, I could ride my bike. It was only twenty miles.

Meanwhile Steve was learning to do proper pruning, and he was spraying and planting more nursery stock. I was busy with farm chores too, and it was a pleasure to be outdoors rather than inside some facility or some airport. And I thought up a number of ways we could improve things while at the same time not wasting money.

The Belchertown dump had always served as my personal Home Depot and I was over there quite a bit, scavenging old bicycle parts to make a honey extractor or baby buggy chassis to recycle into useful things like mobile chicken coops. And you'd be surprised what you can build with an old wheelchair!

As we started to become real farmers, we depended quite a lot on other folks. Farmers always seem ready to lend each other a hand or give advice. There was Preston Atwood, for instance.

We had an old hay bailer, which tended to go down just when we needed it. Of course, we only needed it when we were haying, and then we were generally in a hurry because a storm always seemed to be threatening. Now that I think of it, the bailer wouldn't have gone down when we weren't haying. Oh, well. When we *were* bailing hay and the thing went down, the only person who could fix it was Preston Atwood.

Now Preston worked for the water department, but I don't think he got paid. However, whenever the bailer failed, Steve would have to figure out where the town was digging a sewer and then he'd have to go find Preston. And Preston would leave the sewer right away and come up to the farm and fix the bailer.

And there was Ed Gay who raised goats. He used to take them to the Blandford Fair. It was Ed who got me interested in raising goats myself and who gave me my first taste of goat's milk.

Later on we got to know Carol Hillman and Bob Colness up in New Salem. We'd go up there every year to their Cider Days bash where we'd enjoy the cider made from their heirloom apples.

Steve

We went to the Methodist church, and a lot of the people who helped us out with farming hints and such were Methodists too. Paul Lucier, for instance. I'm not sure he was a Methodist, but nevertheless, he was a great guy. One day he noticed us trying to get hay in before a storm. He just parked his truck and pitched in.

Of course, we tried to do our share of helping out, so from time to time we'd check in on folks who seemed to need a hand. And that's how I happened to be looking in on Louie and Bernice Bellrose. Well, we were just getting our feet wet at farming—this was long before we'd moved up to the orchard—and I figured I could ask them a few farming questions.

The first thing I noticed when I stepped in was a certain smell. You know the smell some old farmhouses have? A smell that suggests there haven't been a lot of changes going on? And maybe some of the food they've been putting up has gone just a bit off? That sort of smell.

Anyway, Louie seemed glad to see me.

"Come in, Steve, come in."

And he waved me in and I followed him down a short hall toward the kitchen. Well, before we got to the kitchen, I sort of glanced to my right, into the Bellroses' bathroom, and there in the bathtub was a calf.

"Louie," I said. "I see you have a calf in your bathtub, why ... what...?"

"Oh," he explained, "we're cooling it."

Well, that didn't explain much to me, but I didn't ask anything more. When I left Louie and Bernice's, I didn't know anymore about calf butchering than I do today, but I suspect it doesn't usually involve a bathtub.

Meg

I like apple orchards. I grew up in one. Our house in Ohio was built on the site of a farm. The original farmhouse was right next door and our backyard had been the farm's orchard. There were still about two dozen productive apple trees, I would guess, most of them Baldwins, those compact, dark-red apples from the olden days.

We picked the apples mostly by climbing the trees. Kind of risky, I guess, but I felt at home in the trees. I'd climb up and do my homework in the crotch of the branches.

My father didn't know anything about pruning apple trees, but he did have the idea that they needed to be sprayed. So he bought a sprayer and four times a season, he and I did the spraying. I enjoyed this. It was my job to pull the sprayer through the orchard while he pointed the nozzle up at the trees and sprayed with enthusiasm. It was like a giant squirt gun fight, and I would have liked to aim the nozzle, but that wasn't my job.

Turns out that my father didn't know much more about spraying than he knew about pruning. Neither of us wore protective gear—masks or hazmat suits. At the end of the orchard, we were soaked and probably wore more spray than the trees did. Oh well, it didn't seem to affect us in the end.

Steve

There's an old saying: "The apple doesn't fall far from the tree." I think that's kind of ironic, considering that these days I think of myself a farmer and an apple grower. I can think back to the first apple tree I knew. It was in our backyard in Ohio, and I'd pick apples and my mother made applesauce and pies. I loved picking those apples—even picking them up off the ground—but I didn't love weeding, and my mother, who was always thinking up chores, thought up that one.

Part of the reason I disliked weeding was because my grandfather supervised me, and he had a lot to say. But he deserved my respect because he had founded Forest City Tree Protection Co. and Nursery, and I felt I had to listen to him.

Eventually, I started my ill-starred college career at The Ohio State University—and here's another irony. It's a land grant school founded to educate farmers. Ohio State failed with me though. I had no idea what I was doing in Columbus and I struggled. My father, trying to help, suggested I go see a friend of his, Professor Chadwick. So I did. I didn't have any idea why I was there and neither did Professor Chadwick,but I eventually did find out that I was sick and tired of drawing cotyledons for his horticulture class. So I spent my days snoozing in the college library, hiding out from Professor Chadwick, and shortly after that, the U.S. Army got ahold of me.

After I'd served my hitch and was a civilian again, my father had another suggestion. This time it was a good one. He recommended the two year associate's program offered by the Stockbridge School of Agriculture at UMass, and that's where I found my stride. I loved Stockbridge and loved the time I spent there, and it inspired me to go to UMass and earn a degree in environmental design.

I was walking through the orchard the other day, sort of reflecting on it all—on the apple tree in Ohio, on my grandfather who founded Forest City Tree, on Stockbridge, on UMass and even on Professor Chadwick—and I thought how my life has come full circle. Here we are, Meg and I, taking care of Sentinel Farm, being stewards of the land for a while. It took some time to get here—and maybe some more time to find out who we are—but now it's pretty clear. We are farmers.

APPLES: THE PRINCIPAL CROP

Steve

I guess apples were the impetus for the farm. We started with apples, and they are Sentinel Farm's principal crop. Apples and apple trees were always part of the landscape in my life— and in Meg's life, too. Furthermore, I grew up in a family of arborists, so Sentinel Farm sort of proves that the apple doesn't fall far from the tree.

Around 1985, when we purchased the Skinners' house and the orchard, the apple trees needed attention. Meg and I were still working at our jobs, but I couldn't stop thinking about how I'd improve the orchard. I could see it in my mind's eye and it was my dream and my goal to create what I saw. But working fulltime, there was no chance we'd do an appropriate job, so for a few years, we just left the orchard alone. Untended, it went downhill fast, and after a while, it got to the point I couldn't even walk back there among the trees.

Meg

That made me mad. It wasn't that he *couldn't* walk through the orchard, it was that he *wouldn't*. He didn't want to. The sight of the trees suffering with scab depressed him.

Steve

That's right. And I knew if we were going to do it right—if we were going to be orchardists—things had to change. Our eight acres had about 150 trees—most of them Macintosh, which twenty-five or thirty years ago was the most popular apple, but we had too many Macs. If we were going to build an orchard, we needed variety. Also, the trees were all standard trees—too large for a good working orchard. So I took a number of them down, and eventually planted 150 more, so today our eight acres support around 300 trees, and that includes peach, pear, and plum trees.

I figure we have about twenty-four varieties of apples. Cortlands—my favorites—Honey Crisps, which have become very popular and Crimson Crisp, which is a hard, very flavorful apple and one I am quite fond of. Among others, we have Red Delicious, Liberty, and several kinds of old apples such as Northern Spy, Baldwins, and Gravensteins.

Meg

We don't sell many Gravensteins because I hoard them for applesauce. They make a beautiful pink applesauce. But don't forget the blueberries. If you're counting up fruit the blueberries are excellent producers.

Steve

And blueberries, right.

Well, fruit trees are susceptible to disease—to fungus and insects—and apple scab is probably an orchard's Number One villain. It is a fungus that has to be treated repeatedly by spraying the leaves. If the fallen leaves have scab and overwinter, the spring rains will release the spores of scab and the cycle starts all over again. Apple scab, if not checked, will split the fruit; it's primarily cosmetic, really, but people don't want to buy scabby fruit.

Now that I think of it, that may not be quite true. I ran a little experiment at a farmers' market a couple of years back. I wanted to see the reaction to less-than perfect fruit, so I put out a bushel with a sign that said "Scabby Apples" and a price that was ridiculously low. I sold out. The whole bushel went, and what's more a couple of folks came by the next week wanting to buy more of those Scabby Apples.

Besides Apple Scab, there's no shortage of orchard pests. Apple Fly Maggot is one. And there's Fire Blight, Brown Blight Rot—that mostly hits the peach crop—and there's Plum Curculio. That's a sort of weevil that attacks the plum trees, as you'd expect from the name, but it affects the apples too. And there's San Jose Scale that is caused by a tiny, hard-shelled insect, and there are mites. The treatment for some of these pests is oil spray that you start using in spring; it suffocates the insects and the eggs. We also do border sprays, including the stonewalls, to kill certain insects that like to live there.

Cleanliness is really the best way to combat the pests that don't walk or crawl or burrow. We chop the dropped leaves, and we're very careful with pruning to prevent overleafage. Also, those prunings can be infected and have to be disposed of carefully, either by chopping or burning. Most of the time, we gather them and put them in the burn pile.

Apple trees are resilient, but peaches and plums are not. Apples can take a tough winter, but the other fruits are fussy. A couple of years ago, we had an astonishing warm-up in late January. We were out sugaring in our shirtsleeves, and the peaches, apparently, decided spring had come and the buds swelled. Then February arrived. The temperature dropped like a stone in a well, and the buds froze. We picked two peaches that year. *Two* peaches out of 60 trees.

Now organic is a subject that comes up time and again. Fruit is probably the hardest crop to grow organically, and even orchards that are certified organic use some sprays.

I'm not sure the general public understands what organic means. Shoppers at farmers' markets ask us constantly if our apples are organic. I say that no, we are not totally organic, but we do practice integrated pest management. This includes things like checking frequently for pests like Apple Maggot. One source we rely on is the UMass Agricultural Extension Service that is very good at sending out warnings and reports at the first whiff of local trouble. Anyone can subscribe to this.

The trouble is, people want spot-free fruit, but that demand is mainly cosmetic. Apple scab doesn't look very pretty, but it only affects the skin of the apple and the fruit itself is usually fine.

At the markets, I use a wooden crate that I tip at a twenty degree angle to display the apples. One day a woman came along, looked over the fruit, picked up a couple apples and asked, "Organic?"

"What are you looking for?" I asked.

"Well, apples that are unblemished. I want perfect apples."

I gave her my integrated pest management spiel, and she continued picking through the apples. She picked up every single one, looked it over, and put most of them down until she had a bag of "perfect" fruit.

I've figured out that people don't really understand organic—to them, it's just another word for pretty.

Another concept about fruit growing that isn't understood is that it's a year-round job. It isn't just pick the fruit in fall and take it to market. An orchardist's year goes something like this:

In December, we watch until the there have been 26 days of freezing weather, and that usually takes us into January. After that, we can start pruning. Well, pruning can start if there's not so much snow that we can't walk in the orchard. Pruning is exhausting work. I keep at it and at it and hope it's done by March.

On Sentinel Farm, pruning time is compromised by maple sugaring. Even before the sap starts running, I have to put aside some of the pruning work and start preparing the sugaring equipment—setting the taps, checking the evaporator and other equipment. Sugaring really cuts into my tree work, and sometimes I resent it. From mid-January until well in March, we're pruning by daylight and boiling sap in the sugarhouse until well into the night. Our son-in-law does most of the night boiling, but the sap has to be collected during daylight. Meanwhile, we're gathering up the prunings and trying to dispose of them.

Meg

We give some to the goats, but even goats can't eat all the stuff Steve takes out of the trees.

Steve

By March the pruning should be done but if it's a good year, we're still boiling syrup like mad. As the weather warms some, I start checking orchard equipment, the sprayer and so forth. And I put down fertilizer.

Meg

My mother was very serious about the orchard. While she was living in Orchard House and Steve and I were still down in the Yellow House, she felt she was in charge. And she felt duty-bound to keep us informed and in line. As the weather warmed and silver tips began to show—that's the first stage of the bud—she became intensely vigilant. She watched and waited for "The Three Old Men." When there are three days of cold, rainy weather in late spring, that's the Three Old Men and when they leave—when the weather clears—it is important to get a dormant oil spray on the trees. She'd be all over Steve about it. "Steve! You'd better get that sprayer going." She could be a real nag about it.

Steve

By the time the trees bloom, I want to have at least one oil spray on and the pruning done and the stuff we've pruned cleaned up and carted away. In bloom time, I'm able to estimate the sort of crop we're going to see. You don't get an apple out of every single blossom, but you can see when it's a heavy blossom year or when it's not and judge accordingly.

This is a critical time now. You have about five days to spray an insecticide that prevents Plum Curculio, and it can be a tight window, that five days of what is called "petal fall."

During petal fall in 2017, however, I found myself—with Meg, of course— off the coast of the Netherlands on a bicycle seat. I was pedaling for all I was worth along the North Sea and thinking the whole time about Plum Curculio and wondering how I'd allowed Meg to convince me to take this trip at this time.

Meg

Well, it was our 50th anniversary that year, and there was this bicycle trip to the Frisian Islands off the Netherlands coast, and I thought "Perfect! The perfect way to celebrate!" So just after New Year's, I booked us into this trip sponsored by the

Vermont Bicycle Club. And I guess Steve wasn't paying attention. Oh well, when you're an apple grower, there's never a good time to be away.

Steve

I complained about it afterward to an old fella who also had an orchard. I knew he'd appreciate the terrible timing.

He considered for a while. And then he said, sort of drawing out his words, "Well... seems to me you'll have a few more petal falls ahead of you, but you and your wife now, you only have one 50th anniversary."

After petal fall, comes a time when things slow down slightly. We'll monitor sticky traps for the appearance of detrimental insects and check for active apple scab on leaves. Then I'll spray when necessary as other pests and fungi show up. On average, we spray about twelve times per season. I also spray to add nutrients like calcium, boron, and zinc. And I might put down lime or send soil samples off to the main campus at the UMass extension.

Weather is critical at any time, and you can't do anything about it except be alert to what's coming and brace yourself. The Extension Service here in Belchertown puts out an online newsletter called *Healthy Fruit Notes* that monitors the weather and offers reminders of what you should be doing and what pitfalls might be working. And it's helpful.

So you do what you can, go over your equipment and hope that your sprayer works. If I'm having trouble with the sprayer, help is available at Orchard Equipment Supply in Conway, Mass. It's the coolest place. They can fix anything, and they understand your need is immediate, so they turn the repairs around fast.

First thing you know, we're into summer pruning when we cut out the new growth and get rid of suckers. And I keep in mind that over-pruning one year will encourage suckers the next year.

By July, we're gearing up for the farmers' markets where we'll be taking the apples, pears, and peaches.

Meg

And blueberries.

Steve

And blueberries. Now our blueberries *are* organic.

By August the early appes are ripening. The Gravensteins, for example, are coming in and Meg is waiting to start applesauce production.

We actively prune our fruit trees all summer. The wisdom used to be "you prune in late winter"—and that's still when we do the major part of it. But new wisdom, it seems, is always supplanting old, and now we thin practically year-round. Summer pruning is mainly removing suckers, and come June, the suckers shoot up. But thinning includes judiciously removing fruit. If our peach trees have had a good bloom, for example, I might pull ten peaches off the trees for every peach I allow to stay and ripen. This practice yields larger fruit as well as a larger crop the following year.

By fall—September, October and into early November— we are very busy picking and working on Pick-UR-Own as well as handling the duties of the farmers' markets.

Columbus Day generally closes the season. Most of the fruit is gone by Thanksgiving. And then we put down our pruning hooks and gathering baskets and rest until its time to start all over again in the new year.

Steve

In the middle of writing this book, I got wind of a new program that was starting out in Stockbridge at my alma mater, the Shade Tree Lab. After more than ten years without a pest management program, UMass was rectifying the situation. Candidates interested in heading up the new program were being interviewed in open sessions, and I planned to attend each one.

After three days of listening, I was enormously pleased that my choice—the very last candidate interviewed—was the person selected. Dr. Jaime Pinero is an entomologist hired by the extension service to research and teach. And he is especially interested in my old nemesis, the Plum Curculio. He said that he was looking for orchardists willing to work with him on his research. I was probably the first in line.

Jaime visited Sentinel Farm on a fine day in early June, and he hung pest pheromone traps in selected apple trees—traps especially designed to attract the Plum Curculio weevil. He took sample counts, and then, for a one-two punch, he treated the ground under the trees with nematodes that will kill the larvae that may be present in fallen apples. According to Dr. Pinero, this treatment could make it possible to cut the spray we use in a single season by 70%. I am hopeful. And I am delighted.

Meg

Nematodes. Good. I always wanted to see a nematode

EVERY FARM NEEDS A HORSE

Meg

It started with one pony. We figured we had the land, so we might as well get some animals. Then too, the girls were small, and they wanted a pony.

I was working as a physical therapist at the Belchertown State School, and since the State School has been gone for many years, I probably should talk a little about it.

The State School was part of the Massachusetts state hospital system, and was focused on developmentally delayed children and adults. Like several of these institutions, the Belchertown State School operated as a working farm. Then, in 1992, Gov. Michael Dukakis shut down almost all the state hospitals, but that is another story, and in my opinion, it's a sad one. The whole story is sad.

Anyhow, while I was at the State School, I became friendly with Candy Dixon, and for the rest of her short life, she led me into some lively adventures. Candy was an equestrian—and a good one—so most of our adventures involved horses.

About the time Steve and I were considering a pony for the girls, Candy Dixon showed up with one. Princess was an "extra" pony, part of the herd at the Belchertown State School. She was a pretty little chestnut Welsh pony with a flaxen mane and tail and a lot of attitude. We found out she had very strong opinions. But she was free, and that was a benefit from Steve's and my points of view.

We didn't have much of a barn for a pony, but we put Princess in the foundation of the old barn, which had no roof. We had no fencing either, so I pounded some stakes into the ground and slipped two old wooden gutters on top of it, and I figured that would work for a fence.

It turned out it didn't. In no time Princess figured out how to get through that fence. When she got out, she usually went right up to the Common where the Catholic Church was located in those days, and she'd stand outside St. Francis and mingle with the worshippers coming out of Mass. Nearly every Sunday morning we'd get a call from the police, and Steve would go up to the Common, say good morning to most of the congregation, and lead Princess home.

That year I turned thirty-five—and by the way, *that* turned out to be the worst year of my life, just about.

I decided I wanted to ride. So I went over to UMass and took a few riding lessons.

However, I was too tall to ride the pony, so I asked Elizabeth Burke to show me how to hitch Princess to a cart and drive.

Now right here I'll explain that Elizabeth Burke is a Scotswoman and from a very elegant, although eccentric, Scottish family. She, Elizabeth, was an excellent rider and she also knew how to drive. So we borrowed a cart from Liesl and Elizabeth tacked up Princess and we were all set. I thought at the time that Elizabeth was sitting kind of funny. She was facing the back of the cart and was sort of driving one-handed. I thought that was unusual, but I didn't think to ask about it.

Things were just fine when we started down the woods trail behind the Yellow House, but then Princess acted up and Elizabeth left the cart. Left it. Just hopped off the back and began running in the other direction—*running*—and I was left trying to hold the situation together. And I didn't make a very good job of it. I finally got Princess under some sort of control, but then I fell down and got stabbed with one of the shafts of the cart, and that was my first broken rib. But at least I learned why Elizabeth Burke was driving backward

I had some other troubles that year. I fell down again while I was walking to the Two Cows to meet friends for lunch, and I cut my knee quite badly. All through lunch my knee bled all down into my sock, and I used up quite a few of the Two Cows's paper napkins mopping and trying to stop the bleeding. I wasn't very successful. And it was kind of embarrassing to keep helping myself to all those paper napkins.

Then I fell off my bike. It was a big old second-hand thing with balloon tires, and I didn't think anybody could fall off one of those. It took seventeen stitches to close up my head, and I was in bed for a week because my eyes were swollen shut and my entire face was level with the end of my nose. They tell me now it was every color in a crayon box. Abby and Molly were quite small that summer and as I lay in bed, I'd sort of hear them in the distance, playing downstairs. Then I'd hear them coming upstairs. I'd hear their sweet little voices and the sweet little voices of their friends who were coming upstairs too. They'd all come into the bedroom and stand beside my bed.

"There she is," I'd hear one of my girls say.

"Wow," their friends would say, impressed. "Oh, wow."

If I'd only thought to charge admission I could have been wealthy by the time my face healed and I was able see again.

Steve

Our next free horse was Goldy. He was a retired circus horse. A Palomino. We could ride Goldy, although with some restraint because he was old and blind. Also he didn't hear well. Riding Goldy was a matter of sitting on him and letting him go where he wanted and that was good because Goldy was very cautious about his footing. He didn't want to fall down, and as a result the rider was quite safe.

Apparently, one of Goldy's circus jobs was counting. His trainer would call out the number thirteen, for example, and Goldy would paw thirteen times with his hoof. We tested him a few times and as far as I could see, he couldn't count up to thirteen. Maybe he could get to three or four. I don't know.

Well, Goldy got so he couldn't find his food and he was blundering around, and I decided he needed to be put down. So I called Dr. Ruder who was a veterinarian in Amherst, and he was known to bend an elbow a bit.

"We have a horse that needs to be put down," I told him. Dr. Ruder knew Goldy, and he agreed.

Then I realized I'd need to put Goldy somewhere after he was put down. So I called a guy I knew on the Belchertown planning board.

"Don," I said, "can you come over with your backhoe and dig a hole? I have a horse that's being put down."

And Don said he would come.

The day started badly. And it didn't improve. For one thing it was hot. Must have been eighty-five or ninety degrees. I had a meeting in Holyoke, and I waited as long as I could before leaving for the meeting, but neither Don nor Dr. Ruder had shown up. So I drove to Holyoke, got through the meeting and got back as fast I could.

Much of the day was used up by then, and I was getting nervous. For one thing, the girls were due back and I didn't want them coming home in the middle of ... well, in the middle of it all.

Just about then Dr. Ruder turned into the drive and drove over the lawn and pulled up with a jerk in front of the Print House. It was obvious he'd had a liquid lunch. A long liquid lunch.

I started walking him down to the pasture where we wanted the deed done, and Ruder lurched along in his suit, carrying his leather doctor bag. You wouldn't have wanted to light a match near him, I'll tell you that.

"What do you want me to do?" I asked him.

"Just hold the halter."

So I held the halter.

Dr. Ruder finally managed to get a syringe out of his bag and get it filled. Then he plunged the needle into the horse's neck, and Goldy sort of staggered, then he collapsed. I leaned over to have a look at him, and he emitted an immense sound of escaping gas. I jumped back and Ruder leaned over to have a look himself, and Goldy repeated the expletive. Ruder's reaction was the same as mine.

"Better give him another shot," Ruder mumbled.

After the second shot, it was clear that Goldy was resting in peace.

Don showed up and finished the job and I was relieved because the flies were gathering in the blistering heat. The kids were due any second and I didn't want to do any explaining to *them*.

Meg

When you have horses, you have to feed them, so that's how we started growing our own hay.

Our hay field was on a slope. A slope of at least forty-five degrees. Maybe more. Well, we needed hay for the horses and

SO WE BECAME FARMERS

you do the best you can with what you have. So at haying time, we made it a family affair, and all four of us turned out.We had a '52 Ford in those days. It wasn't registered, so we couldn't put it on the road, but it was fine for driving around the hayfield.

Once the hay was bailed, one of us would heave it into the truck bed, assisted sort of by the two small girls, and the other one of us would drive the truck, moving it along slowly to the spots where there was hay that had to be thrown.

Steve and I eventually figured out that this wasn't the best use of available labor. With two adults throwing instead of just one, we reasoned that we could be considerably more productive.

So we looked at Abby. She was about eleven. And we taught her to drive the Ford. Abby wasn't happy about it, and she complained from time to time, but she was good at driving. She learned to handle the clutch, the brake and the standard shift, and she could do it all on a slope. Moreover she rarely stalled the thing.

Well, that was fine.

Then we reviewed our division labor once again. Abby was a good worker. And she was strong. So we asked ourselves, wouldn't she be more useful on the ground?

Well, yes.

Then we turned around slowly and looked at Molly. She was about nine. And she was kind of small for her age. But never mind that, Steve taught Molly to drive the Ford.

She didn't drive as well as Abby. She tended to stall out more often, and she was too small to see through the windshield. She had to crane her neck through the open side window, but she was determined.

So with Molly driving and the rest of us loading, we brought in the hay crop and fed the horses through the winter.

After Goldy was gone, we eventually ended up with three

horses, all with names that began with the letter "P", and things got a little confusing.

There was Princess, of course, the Welsh pony. And then Prancer came. And eventually there was Petunia.

Now Prancer was a wonderful horse. I think he was a Morgan. He'd been living over in Ware in a breezeway. Actually, it was just someone's screened porch that connected their house to a garage. I don't know how the breezeway woman and Prancer got connected, but I do know that he, Prancer, had shipping fever. The woman who owned the horse had to get him out of the breezeway and so, with the shipping fever and the breezeway urgency, we got him for not much money at all. And Prancer came to the Yellow House in Belchertown.

Prancer really taught me to ride. I learned more from him than I did from those lessons at UMass. I'd go out trail riding with Pat Fuller, Elizabeth Burke, and Anne Cann, and we'd have the best time. Prancer loved to gallop, but he didn't like to stop, and the only way I could control him was to pull up behind somebody else so he had to stop.

Candy Dixon liked the look of Prancer, and it wasn't long before she came up with the idea of starting a therapeutic riding venture for disabled individuals in the community who didn't reside at the State School. Candy would be the horse expert and I had the pediatric therapy knowledge, and as Candy described it, with our qualifications we couldn't miss.

So back along our woods road behind the Yellow House, Steve and I built a ring with a ramp. One day a week we'd give therapeutic riding lessons there and on one other day, I'd truck Princess and Prancer over to Candy's house to work in her ring.

Steve

Candy Dixon had known Princess from her days at the Belchertown State School, but there was another kind of horse

54

that would be, according to Candy, the "perfect" therapy horse—a Norwegian Fjord pony. So we found an eighteen-month-old filly, brought her home and named her Petunia. She was a breed you don't commonly see, but she was easy to train and fit in well.

The Fjord has a distinctive look. It's a type of type of draught horse, but smaller and with greater agility. It has a compact body and a thick, strong-looking neck. It seems to be all muscle and bone, it's capable of carrying a fully-grown adult, and it can pull good-sized loads. The color is distinctive too. All Fjords are dun and in winter, the coat gets really heavy. The mane is long and thick so it's usually clipped, giving the horse a sort of punk-rock look. As far as I can tell, from my long association with them, Fjords are gentle and have calm dispositions. I suppose that's why Candy Dixon thought Petunia would work out well in the therapeutic riding scheme that she and Meg were working out.

Well, I was kind of interested in Petunia because, in the back of my mind, I always felt a horse could do a lot of the farm work. I pictured the horse hauling cordwood and piles of brush and so forth. In some ways, a horse is better than a tractor, because the horse can move along with you as you do the chores and it stands there when it's told to, and you don't have to keep hopping up and down from a tractor. So while we were collecting horses, I kept that pulling/driving thing in the back of my mind.

I'll come back to it later. But first I'd like to talk a little about one of the downsides of horse ownership. Our horses kept escaping.

Princess kept breaking out and going to the Common to hang around with the Catholics. After while everyone knew her and knew where she belonged so it wasn't that much of a problem when she went AWOL

Or it hadn't been, up to the time Meg and I went to Erie to attend a family funeral. Fortunately, Meg's mother was visiting, and she was happy to stay with Abby and Molly. So we were all set.

Then Princess made another jailbreak while we were in Erie, and this time she took Petunia with her. They got as far as the State School, which was her alma mater, but the State School is several miles from Cottage Street and they crossed Route 202 at least once. Anyhow, they joined the herd down at the farm where they were promptly picked on and beaten up.

Eventually someone figured out where they lived and Meg's mother and Abby and went down and led the horses home.

Dr. Morcom came over to fix them up and he claimed later that he'd hardly been able to get the needle through Petunia's hide to put in the necessary sutures.

"Toughest hide I ever saw," he said.

Well, that's a Fjord, for you.

Prancer got out one night when I was the only one home. Meg and the girls were away on a camping trip with the Girl Scouts or something. I was dead to the world when the phone rang. I made my way downstairs in my birthday suit to the front hall and picked up the phone on the ninth or tenth ring. It was Candy's friend Wayne calling. He wanted to know if our horse was loose.

I had no idea. I barely knew who I was.

Suddenly the front hall was flooded with light and two cops with flashlights blazing peered in.

"I'll just...well, I'll just get some clothes on and then I'll...well I'll just look for the horse," I told them.

I didn't have to look far. Prancer was standing on the front lawn.

I wondered if other horses in Belchertown got out with

such regularity.

Not long after that, we had to put Princess down. She was in a lot of trouble and we found out later that her intestines had wrapped around her stomach. It's not uncommon when horses get down and roll, but surgery is about the only thing that can help and surgery wasn't in the cards.

Dr. Morcom came over again and helped us out and we put Princess down in the pasture where Goldy was buried. Now we had two dead horses on the property.

Meg

Candy Dixon was right. Petunia was an excellent therapy horse. She was gentle, she never spooked and a child with any degree of disability was safe on her back. The only thing was, Petunia's back was so broad that the riders' little legs stuck straight out to the sides, but they didn't care. They gripped her punk-rock mane and were thrilled with their horse.

Candy and I attracted a lot of clients, and before we thought it through, we found ourselves setting up a 501(c)3 non-profit corporation. Pioneer Valley Therapeutic Riding, it was called, and Joann Bernhart came in as a third partner. Pioneer Valley was one of the first such outfits in Western Massachusetts and probably in the state.

The riding part was fine. Candy was an excellent teacher and the kids loved her. As a physical therapist, I understood individual needs and how the action of the horse was able to relax the stiff hip muscles of some of the young riders. Anyhow, the program was very successful. However, neither Candy nor I liked the paperwork that went along with being a non-profit and we weren't very good at it. And we were constantly having to fund-raise to keep the program going. I didn't enjoy that much either.

A lot of work goes into a fund-raising trail ride. The course has to be laid out and marked the day before. Parking for all those trailers has to be arranged. Porta-potties have to be rented. Well, I could go on. But the big thing was the responsibility of it all.

We were holding a fifteen-mile event in Leverett—I'll never forget it. The parents of one of the therapy kids suddenly decided they'd like to ride too. Barb and Ev. Neither of them had ridden for years, but they rented a couple of horses from a livery stable in the forest, climbed into the saddles and promptly got lost. The worse of it was, the woman—Barb—was a serious diabetic and she hadn't taken proper precautions. When we realized they were out there somewhere, wandering hopelessly through the forest, panic set into my chest. I thought I might be having a heart attack. We found them eventually, but Barb didn't look good. Frankly, she looked pretty bad.

By the time one of these events ended, I'd be exhausted. All I'd want to do was go home and open a beer. But I never wanted to go home as badly as I did at the event we held in the Wendell State Forest. The event finally ended—and no one had gotten lost—and the riders were loading their horses into trailers. Now usually there is at least one horse that doesn't want to load, and that day was no exception. Nobody could make that animal walk up the ramp. All the tricks known to all the equestrians were tried and all failed.

It was getting dark. I was cold. I wanted, in the worst way, to go home, and I could see that the horse was never going into that trailer. I was desperate. Then I had an idea.

I knew someone who lived in the town of Wendell, so I drove into town to speak to her. I asked her if she had room in her barn for a horse that wouldn't load, and if we could just get him as far as her barn, would she stable him for the night? Well, she said yes. So I carried the good news back to the owner of the stubborn horse—she was still there beside the trailer with a couple other good souls—and she walked the horse over to Wendell, I guess. I don't know. I went home.

I don't know what happened the next day either. I guess the horse decided to load. I never found out. And I didn't ask.

Steve

I must have said something about wanting to drive a team within the hearing of my brother Rick, because he offered me his Amish meadow buggy. Well, I figured that would be useful on a farm. I didn't let myself be discouraged by Meg's short career driving Princess. I just didn't associate it with anything I might run into at all.

The meadow cart needed some work, so I took it to Jim Chevalier, right here in Belchertown. Jim is an expert at restoring carts and buggies. He had, in fact restored a buggy for none other than Whoopi Goldberg, althouth I sometimes wondered what Whoopi would do with it. Anyhow, I told him I was planning to drive Petunia and sell apples out of the cart.

"Oh. Well," he said, "This cart is in tough shape. I'm going down to Pennsylvania Amish country pretty soon, and I can get you something much better than *this* cart."

And before long I got a call from Jim.

"I found just what you want," he said.

When I got down to his shop, I discovered he'd gotten an Amish buggy, not a cart. Well, okay, I paid him and hauled the buggy home.

I'd seen a lot of those buggies when I was growing up and had risked life and limb trying to pass them on the country roads of northeastern Ohio. When I got my own buggy, I could see why the Amish had gone to fiberglass in the last few years. For one thing those old buggies rusted out from road salt.

We had some Amish tack around the place—I'd been collecting it toward the day when I'd have something to drive.

Meg and I had done some land driving—that's where you harness the horse and walk alongside—and we'd taken Prancer, and then Petunia, through the orchard that way, hauling wood or pulling the stone boat, and things had gone pretty well. But to really get the feel of the thing, I went down to Monson to attend a driving school.

The season turned and it got to be winter. And we had a sleigh. And then we got a good round of snow. Perfect. I tacked up Prancer and hitched him to the sleigh, and we started down the driveway. We couldn't go onto the street, of course, because there was no snow on the street—plows and salt had taken care of that—but I figured we could drive along the sidewalk. And we started out, heading up toward the Common.

We'd only gone a short way when Prancer started picking up speed. Then more speed. And I started slipping off the seat and when he hit a gallop, I fell off entirely. And there was Prancer, galloping, and there I was looking up at the sky, watching the telephone poles whip past. I still had hold of the reins, although I don't know how. Well, I finally hauled myself back up into the seat and managed to get Prancer slowed down to a trot, then to a walk. He was hardly out of breath, but I couldn't say the same for myself.

Once we had the Amish buggy, we would occasionally drive it up to the Common with Petunia pulling, and that always caused interest and comment. We changed the Sentinel Farm logo to include the Amish buggy with our big red apple on the door to advertise the farm.

After Prancer went to his reward, Petunia was our only horse. Horses are herd animals and really shouldn't live alone. So we looked around for another Fjord and eventually, up in Danbury, New Hampshire, we found Sole. He was extremely gentle but I don't think he was too bright. He reminded me of one of Garrison Keillor's Norwegian bachelor farmers. Sole adapted well to Sentinel Farm though, and he followed Petunia all around the pasture and the orchard, and he listened to her when she told him what to do.

We could see that Petunia and Sole would make a handsome team, and so our interest in driving took an uptick. Sam White, our orchard manager from way back, had quite a bit of experience driving workhorses, and he offered to come and show us the ropes. Or the reins, in this case. So he came over and we got the Fjords harnessed and hitched.

"Get on up here," he said to me, and we set off down the orchard.

I wasn't comfortable. Not a bit. I was thinking about Elizabeth Burke positioning herself to jump off the pony cart at the first hint of trouble, and I wished I were riding backward. It seemed it would be much safer because Sam had those horses going at what felt to me like thirty miles an hour.

The lesson ended after what seemed like hours, and Sam went home. Meg and I kept at it though, and I have to say, when Sole and Petunia were all tacked up in their Amish harnesses with the leather hearts across their chests, they made a handsome team. They were a good advertisement for Sentinel Farm.

When you have workhorses, you have to *work* them. Everyday. Although we were well intentioned, we eventually did some backsliding, and so our team never achieved what it might have. We went back to using the meadow cart and eventually, when we started the Pick-UR-Own operation, we'd take visitors on tours around orchard with Petunia pulling. It was quite an attraction.

Meg

What I learned from therapeutic riding was how to drive a horse trailer—how to turn around and how to park and how to back up. For a long time after that, the only vehicle I had in my own name was the horse trailer. I didn't have a car or a truck with my name on the registration, and I thought if there were ever a divorce, I'd be stuck. But when someone found the cow, it was good that I had the horse trailer,

The cow was living over on Warner Road, living under a tree, but there was a stream nearby. The property was about to be turned into a housing development, so of course the cow couldn't continue living alone on Warner Road. And somebody—well, it wasn't really the owner, but she thought she was the owner, sort of, because she and the cow had developed a relationship. Zoe. Her name was Zoe. The cow's name, according to Zoe, was Daisy. I didn't know Zoe at the time. But she visited the cow every day and fed her donuts.

Well, Zoe realized the cow had to move and I guess she asked around to find out who might have a trailer, and I was the one they found. I had a trailer, but I had to convince Steve to hook the trailer up to his truck. Finally he said yes, but he wasn't happy about it, and he made it very clear that Daisy could not come to our house. That cow was the last thing we needed, he said.

I took my problem to my friend Joanna Page, who will help just about anything or anybody in need, and she said that the cow could come and stay at her house, but just until I could convince Steve that we could keep Daisy.

So Steve hitched up my horse trailer to his truck and we drove over to Warner Road where Zoe was waiting with Daisy. We got Daisy into the trailer by luring her with donuts. Then I got in the front seat of the truck with Steve, and Zoe climbed into the back where she had a good view of the trailer, and off we went.

But not very far.

From the back of the truck we heard Zoe holler, "Hold it!

Stop! Hold it!"

Steve looked in his side mirror and saw that the whole side of the trailer was bulging like somebody inside had blown up a huge balloon.

He held up.

"Get back there and fix it," he said to me. He said it through his clenched teeth.

When Zoe and I got back there. We found the cow had shifted and was standing crosswise in the trailer. Of course, we had to turn her around so she'd be front-to-back, only she wasn't wearing a halter, so turning her was hard to do.

Finally Zoe and I both grabbed her head and wrenched her around by sort of lifting her up, but there was nothing we could do for the trailer. It was in tough shape. The side still bulged and the axle was damaged.

Daisy's stay over at Joanna's was short. She ate a number of the Christmas trees that Joanna sells each December. Then she broke out of the pen Joanna and I had cobbled together and ate quite a number of the Pages' prize perennials.

Alan Page joined Steve in banning cows from their premises, and I called a man up on Gulf Road. Beauregard was his name. He said he'd take Daisy. She went up to Gulf Road and was never seen again.

THE CHICKEN OR THE EGG?

Meg

We were trying to think the other day, which came first? Our chickens or the coop? I'm pretty sure it was the coop. I'd been wanting to build a mobile chicken coop ever since I read about a rig that could be moved around the property and would keep the birds safe from predators.

Steve

Meg was interested in designing and building the coop, but I didn't in any way discourage her. Chickens are beneficial. They eat grubs and ticks and other bugs and nuisances on a farm, and while they are pecking away, they are also dropping manure that enriches the soil. It's a win-wing venture.

Meg

I built the first mobile chicken coop on a wheelchair frame, which was probably a mistake. But I had several old frames left from the days of *SEEK (Special Equipment Exchange*

Katalog), an idea I had to help cash-strapped parents of special needs children by re-circulating and recycling equipment. I've built quite a few things on those frames, but I've pretty much used them up by now.

Anyhow, that first coop wasn't a great success. The wheelchair was tippy. We weren't keeping any chickens at the time, but Dave and Abby were. So I went down to their house and borrowed half a dozen hens, brought them up to Sentinel Farm and stuffed them into my wheelchair-coop. Then a pair of foxes climbed all over the coop, tipped it and ate the chickens.

Well, you can't expect to always get it right the first time.

Next I went to the Belchertown dump. I've mentioned the dump before. It's sort of my version of Home Depot, except its closer and the stuff I "shop" for is free. I brought home every bicycle frame the dump had.

Now the only parts I wanted off these bikes were the front wheels. Picture it. There's a front wheel that is held in place with a fork. I sawed off all the forks on all the bicycles and saved the rest of the chasses in case I thought up something useful for them later on.

My friend Marc, a co-piper in the Quabog Highlanders, got all charged up about the plan when I told her about it. She's an architect, and she drew some very professional plans for the mobile coop. She did a cross section and a longitudinal elevation and a framing plan, and she included detail for a custom weld and detail of the custom nesting boxes—oh, it was all very elaborate.

I took the wheels and forks and the plans to our friend Leo, who is a talented welder, although he usually works on hotrods, and he welded oarlock things onto the forks so that they could attach to the sides of the wooden coops. Then I rummaged a pair of saplings out of Steve's brush pile and pushed these through the oarlocks to form wagon staves that would allow me to pull the coop from place to place. So the coop was standing there on its two wheels, and I fashioned a chicken wire pen on the front, so the hens could hop down a little chicken ramp and be protected during the day from predators in whatever patch of real estate they found themselves. At night, we remembered to shut the chickens up inside.

This newer model of mobile coop was so successful, that I built a second one for our daughter Molly, and we hauled that up to Hancock, New Hampshire where Molly and her family were living at the time. They've moved on, but I believe the coop is still in Hancock and still in use.

So, we had our own flock of chickens, of course. And they lived in the coop and got moved regularly when they had wiped out the ticks and grubs in one area and had nicely manured their premises.

Eventually the chickens got tired of moving, I guess. They must have held a meeting of sorts and everyone voted and decided among themselves to make one last move. All together, they moved into the barn cellar and refused to be persuaded back to the coop. So the barn has been their permanent address for the last eight or nine years. During the day, they range freely through the gardens and the orchard, but at night, they get shut up safely in the barn.

Steve

Our flock ebbs and swells. Predators are always out there — foxes, coyotes, hawks. One time I saw a big hawk swoop down and sink its talons into the back of a hen. But then, the hen proved too heavy, and the hawk couldn't achieve lift-off. The two of them struggled along, both flapping like mad and the chicken squawking for all she was worth. But she was just too much load for the hawk. Eventually he got his talons loose and sailed off, and the chicken didn't seem too much worse for her episode.

On another day I was privileged to witness a coyote grab a chicken and head off toward the woods. And there came Meg, running right along behind, and she was mad!

"Let go of that chicken!" she was hollering. "You drop that chicken right now!"

The coyote looked back over his shoulder—and Meg was coming along—and damned if he didn't drop it! And he was picking up speed as he headed for the woods.

Meg's hens are productive—I'll give them that. And the eggs they lay are large, with yolks that stand right up, bright orange and practically bursting with nutrition. They make grocery store eggs look pale and whimpy in comparison.

We have Araucanas, Rhode Island Reds, Black Sex-link, and once upon a time, we had a Suffollk hen ...

Meg

Yes, we had a Suffolk. And we also had a neighbor just down the hill. Jackie was her name, and she was a certified East Coast Poultry judge. She kept a number of prize hens and she kept them in luxury. Radiant heat in the coop floors. Things like that.

Anyway, Jackie came over one day for something or other and as she was crossing the yard, she spotted the Suffolk hen— of course we didn't know then it was a Suffolk—but Jackie stopped short.

"Oh my goodness," she said, "Just look at that! What a beautiful chicken!"

Well, she told us it was a Suffolk and she went on and told us all about the breed. It is among the oldest of the British chicken breeds, we found out. The eyes are red and so are the earlobes. I remember she said that. I never knew chickens had earlobes. It's funny, the things you find out when you're just standing in your yard. Anyhow, Jackie thought our chicken could be a prize-winner at the New England chicken show which was going to be held at the Eastern States Exhibition in Springfield.

She carried on so, Jackie did, that I finally agreed to take the chicken to Springfield. And I was supposed to wash its feet and do some other stuff to prepare it for the event.

When we got to the Exhibition, Jackie took over. She had a little square make-up bag and she got busy with the chicken. She polished its beak; she polished its toenails; she fluffed up its feathers and then she got some stuff out of the make-up bag and applied *that*. That chicken had on more make-up than I wore when I was a mother-of-the-bride.

Steve and I stood around for a while and watched the chicken. It was in a cage with immaculate sawdust. But eventually we got tired of standing around looking at the chicken standing in the sawdust, so we went home and missed the judging.

The chicken won a prize. First prize. Jackie was so proud when she brought the chicken home with its award. We photographed the chicken and put the award on the mantel, and everybody congratulated everybody else. And Jackie went home.

And the next week a fox caught that prize chicken and ate it.

"*Sic transit gloria mundi*," my brother-in-law, Don Doyle, murmured when he got the news.

GETTING OUR GOATS

Steve

I didn't want to learn about raising goats for the same reason Meg didn't want to learn how to prune fruit trees. If you don't know how to do a thing, you can't be called upon to do it. In fact, now that we have the electric pruner, Meg does some of the basic pruning, and I—well, I have gotten involved to some extent in goat raising. But the goats, along with the hens, are basically Meg's farm projects.

Meg

I talked about Daisy, the abandoned cow, at the end of the horse chapter. I was interested in Daisy because I was interested in milk production. Daisy was well past her milking prime, but Dr. Morcom thought he could give her some shots and ...well...it simply was not to be.

Daisy became history, but my interest in milk production remained keen. And I thought about goats.

Before I hauled my entire family off to the Blandford Fair

to learn more about goats and have my first drink of actual goat milk, we had Marigold.

She was given to me as a going-away gift. The staff at the Belchertown State School was bailing out left and right as part of Gov. Dukakis's closing program, and finally I decided to leave too. The few people who were left in my department put their heads together and came up with an ideal gift, and the gift turned out to be Marigold. I was thrilled. She was a black and white Nubian, she was absolutely beautiful, and she didn't realize she was a goat.

We were living down at the Yellow House then. Abby and Molly were young and Marigold assumed she was just another sister. She played with the girls. Tried to do everything they did. She'd go mad with delight when they played on their swings. She was right in the middle of everything we did, and she would not—*would not*—stay in her pen. She'd take a running leap at the stonewall and from there, jump to freedom. It upset her when we went inside the house because she couldn't join us. She'd look in all the windows, stand on the picnic table and make an awful fuss. And she refused to hang out with other animals. *We* were her herd.

One of the things I learned about goats from Marigold is that they are herd animals. You shouldn't just try to keep a single goat.

Marigold met a very sad end. Steve and I had gone up to help Arlan Skinner cut some wood and Marigold, naturally, came along too. While we were busy cutting, Marigold was busy eating laurel which is poisonous to goats. There was nothing we could do to save her.

Well, the Blandford Fair was coming and I was determined to be there. A fellow we knew from church—Eddie Gay— was planning to show his goats. Alpine Standards. I rounded up the family, including my mother, Steve's father, my sister and brother-in-law and the girls, of course, and we drove to Blandford. We drove straight up, it seemed. Blandford sits at a high elevation.

Eddie Gay was there, and he was dressed all in white—anyone who shows an animal at a fair is supposed to dress in white. It's a 4H rule or something. But after the showing, Eddie offered me my first taste of warm goat's milk.

Well, that was it. I knew someday I'd have goats.

As I started looking for the beginning of a herd, I "shopped" on *Finder* where there was quite a listing of free goats. Listen. They were free because they each had "something." Something that you probably didn't want to deal with. And free wasn't entirely true either because there was usually an adoption fee, plus any difficulty that turned out to be the result of the "something".

I'd been reading up on goats. Studying. And the main thing I knew was that I wanted a goat that didn't have "something."

So I studied some more.

Then, about eight years ago—and after a lot of research—Steve and I drove up to Orange, and bought a Nigerian Dwarf doe. Mary.

Mary's size was a selling point. We had started the Pick-UR-Own operation, and I figured goats would be a draw. But large goats can be intimidating, especially to small children, and I'd also learned that a dwarf can yield almost as much milk as a larger goat.

We acquired two neutered bucks along with Mary: Sampson, who was lazy, and Franklin, who was...well... Franklin was the sort of goat that qualified as "something." I'll get to Franklin later.

With Mary, the goat business got underway. I intended to breed her, raise a couple of her kids and the milk production would then begin.

Steve

Breeding. This is the where I became involved in goat raising. Meg lined up a woman who had a buck, and I was enlisted to drive Mary up to be bred. I was new to this stuff, and I assumed I'd drop Mary off and she'd be put in a pen with the buck. Then, after a few days, when the deed was done, I'd drive back, pick up Mary and we'd wait 145 days for the kids to arrive.

Then I was told this was to be a "driveway" breeding. Not only did I not understand what that was, I misunderstood the term and thought we were having a "drive by" breeding. Of course, I didn't know what that would be either.

I can't remember where Meg was. And this was her project, by the way, but all I remember now is that she wasn't there. I suppose she had a good excuse though.

So when we arrived, I escorted Mary out of the backseat of my truck, and the goat breeder brought around her buck.

"I gotta go somewhere," she said to me.

"Wait!" I told her, "What do I do? Can't you just..."

"Oh, just hold her leash," the breeder said, "Let them get used to each other. I'll be right back."

And then and there, in the driveway, the buck got right to it. Once. Twice. A third time. I was impressed, and that was it.

I put Mary back in the truck. Now. Here's a goat fact. A buck is a nasty thing. For one thing, it pees on its own beard. Believe it or not, this is supposed to appeal to the doe. Well, the odor that Mary brought back into the truck was something appalling. I drove home with all the windows open.

Meg

For about four months after a goat is bred—and after you establish that the breeding took—there's not much to do concerning the goat. But close to 139 days, I began to grow anxious about being a goat midwife.

For one thing I thought I should be present, and to be sure I would be, I bought a baby monitor. As the time got near, I put the transmitter in the goat pen and the other half on the dresser in our bedroom. Every time I heard a strange noise—a whuffling sound or pawing or thumping—I woke up, and of course woke up Steve. And I'd fly out to the barn where everything always looked the way it always did. Normal. I'd go back to bed. But later that night, and during the next nights, this routine repeated and Steve complained. Finally I shut the monitor off altogether.

Mary chose to deliver at high noon one day. It figures. After I'd bought that baby monitor. I certainly didn't know how I was going to help, but I was standing by.

My friend Susan Andrade was standing by too, and she knew less than I did, but at least she dressed for the role. And I remember remarking on this because Susan is one of those immaculately turned out women whom I admire and will never become.

So Susan and I crouched there in the shavings and straw.

"What'd you think?"

"I don't know."

Steve looked in on us once as we were crouching.

"What happens if it gets stuck or something?" he said.

"I suppose we'll reach in and turn it." I told him.

He didn't look in again.

Mary managed the birth all by herself, and now, counting Franklin and Sampson, I had five goats—the start of a real herd. And I started the tradition of naming the kids for the products of Sentinel Farm. Twins Beauregard and Carolina Ruby, eventually came along, and were named for my favorite varieties of sweet potato. Hubbard, Butternut and Acorn referenced squashes we grow. Lola's triplets were named for three grades of maple syrup, and Amber, Fancy, and Robust were soon dancing around the goat pen. I named one litter for trees on the farm. Acer, of course, for our maples (*Acer saccharum*), and brothers Prunus and Pinus in honor of the farm's principal products because *Prunus* is a genus of all fruit trees (plums, peaches, cherries nectarines and so forth) and any conifer belongs to the genus *Pinus*.

Well, it amused me.

Steve

Another "goatscape" that involved me, also involved Pinus and Prunus. As Meg said, they were brothers but Pinus was a runt. Nevertheless, a woman came to buy a kid and she fell in love with Pinus. But the little guy failed to thrive and after a time, she called Meg, wondering what to do. Meg took the kid back and made an appointment with our vet.

Now Dr. Jess is something of a goat expert, and she is dear to Meg who has known her since she was a child. So Meg was getting ready to take Pinus to Dr. Jess when she had the idea to take Prunus along for company.

It wasn't her best idea.

I was drafted to go along and take care of Prunus. That wasn't a good idea either.

While Dr. Jess was holding Pinus and beginning to examine him, Prunus escaped. Everyone started running around, trying to catch him because the vet's office faces a busy street, and we hadn't even made it inside yet, but Prunus weaved and backed and ducked and was outwitting all comers.

Then I had an idea.

I said I'd go home and get another goat—Hubbard—a goat that Prunus was fond of. Hubbard, I argued, was the one to catch the runaway goat. And I got in the truck got out of there before anyone thought up a counter argument.

And by the time I got back with Hubbard, Prunus had

run into a paddock full of racehorses and allowed himself to be captured.

Meg

I said I was going to talk about Franklin, and now I'm ready. If Franklin had been listed on *Finder*, he would have been one of the goats with "something." We should have called him Houdini. He could get out of any place, anywhere, and we spent a lot of time trying to catch him and pen him up again so he could escape and we could start the routine all over. He was strong though, Franklin. We used to harness him up and he'd pull things.

Franklin was a handful and a headache. I gave him away once. Threw him in as a bonus with a goat I'd sold, but Franklin only lasted a week in his new home and I got him back.

We struggled along with Franklin for a while longer, catching him, putting him in a stronger, cleverer pen, and then seeing him escape again.

Finally, I advertised him on *Craig's List*.

"Goat. Cheap. $50.00, but he can't be contained."

Believe it or not, a woman came along and paid the fifty dollars and she took Franklin home. I didn't even deposit the cash because I figured I'd have to give it back when she returned Franklin.

Sure enough, after a few weeks, I heard from her.

"You were right," she said. "He can get out of anything."

So I braced myself for what I figured was coming.

"But he's a cool goat," she said. "He goes everywhere with me. He takes walks with me. And he comes inside and we watch TV together."

I tried to picture it. Old Franklin sitting right there on the sofa.

Just goes to prove...there's something for everyone.

Steve

If you're going to get goat's milk—and that was Meg's plan— you have to breed the goat. And after that, naturally, comes the kid, and usually a couple of kids because Nigerians generally have multiple births. And you share the doe's milk with the kids until they are weaned and after that, it's all yours.

Meg looks the kids over and sells a few and keeps some of the others, but either way, there are two things you have to do with young kids and both involve me. You have to disbud them and neuter them.

A goat will start sprouting horns almost immediately. Both genders will, and these horns should be nipped in the bud the sooner the better. I suppose that's where the expression came from.

Well, we read up on this process, and we looked at a few YouTube videos. (I recommend looking at a few of these for sheer entertainment value). And after our research, Sentinel Farm purchased a disbudding tool for us. It looks something like the wood burner I learned to use in seventh grade. The idea is to apply the hot iron to the bud, hold it there for several agonizing seconds (agonizing for the kid and for the dis- budder). Nobody enjoys this.

I built a disbudding box—a narrow box into which the kid is inserted and its head is put through a hole at one end of the box. Meg's job was to hold the head still, and my job...well, I was the disbudder. First, I test the tool's heat on a 2x4 while I take a few deep breaths, and when it's hot enough, I fit it onto the bud and hold it for the count of twelve seconds. There is noise and smell and argument over whether it was twelve seconds or only ten, and when this all calms down, Meg gets a better grip on the head and we do the other horn.

It is emotionally exhausting. And it is easy to do a less- than-good job. The do-over isn't any fun either.

There's more work to be done at the goat's other end. Fortunately, not every kid needs neutering, only the males, but every season there's a little waiting list of boys that need attention.

Like disbudding, there is a tool for this. A crimper is our choice. Some breeders band the testicle, but that is inhumane. Some simply pay for the vet to do the deed. But our vet charges $60 to neuter a kid and when you sell the goat for seventy dollars, there isn't much profit, so at Sentinel Farm, it's the crimper. All you need to know is it's sort of like vice grips.

The first time we did this, things got involved.

First, we decided on a division of labor. Meg was going to sit in a low chair and hold the animal. She would grasp the two front legs with one hand, grasp the back legs with the other hand, and would hold the kid against herself, so as to present the target area and make it available to the Crimper.

I was the Crimper, and I would stand at the ready.

To prepare ourselves for the event, we invited our friend Julie Jonassen to participate because Julie is a professor of physiology at UMass Medical and she knows a lot about kidneys and genetic disorders, and she was going to help identify the *vas deferens*.

Julie's husband Rick Rabe joined the surgical team as videographer.

Susan Andrade, looking for a role to play, was the designated timer. The crimp needs to be held for the count of three to five seconds.

Manny Andrade, Susan's husband, decided to stay home. I envied him.

Julie and Rick had recently traveled to France, where Julie had purchased some kind of numbing lotion that she planned to rub on the testicles.

The operation began. Julie rubbed on the lotion. She

massaged for quite a while.

"For gosh sakes, Julie..." I said.

Rick filmed.

I finally found the *vas deferens* and Julie confirmed it.

Susan counted.

"Woo-uu-nnn ... too-oo-whoo..."

"For god's sake, Susan," I said, "get on with it!"

"What? I'm just counting..."

Rick filmed.

We did it.

We've neutered quite a few kids by now with something like a seventy-five percent success rate. I'm not much good at it. Somewhere along the way, we switched roles. Now I'm the holder and Meg is the crimper. It works better this way.

Meg

I sell quite a few goats on the hoof, and that's a nice little profit center for Sentinel Farm, but the point of the whole endeavor was the goat's milk. I'm not allowed to sell goat's milk, but I use it for ice cream and cheese and soaps. Steve and I are fond of the milk, which is sweeter than cow's milk and is naturally homogenized. People who are lactose intolerant can often handle goat's milk. I refrigerate it immediately after milking and there is absolutely no "goaty" taste.

I tried several milking approaches but settled on a hand held milk machine that works quite well. Mary, my matriarch goat, is an excellent breeder but not a terrific milker.

Lola, one of Mary's daughters, is incredibly lazy. She is almost too lazy to push out her kids, but she is an excellent milker.

When the kids are born, we share the milk and I only milk once a day; I close the babies away during the night and milk in the mornings and then the babies can feed all day. When they are weaned, of course, the milk is all mine.

I enjoy making goat milk soap because I feel like a chemist doing experiments. I find the recipes online. I add lye to the frozen the milk, which heats it, and then add the slightly warmed oils, scents, and any pretty bits such as lavender or marigold. An immersion blender churns it all up, and when it's the consistency of pudding, I pour the soap into molds.

I worked through a number of experiments before I could turn out a credible goat cheese, but I've gotten so I can put out a plate of goat cheese and crackers with some pride.

Sentinel Farm has an entire line of goat milk products as well as goats on the hoof. And it is pleasant to look out the sunroom windows at the pen full of goats. And when people come for Pick-UR-Own—and when the kids are dancing and playing—it is quite an attraction.

SWEET STUFF:
MAPLE SUGARING

Meg

We were still living down at the Yellow House when we tapped a few of our sugar maples and boiled the sap to make our first maple syrup. We hung a couple dozen metal buckets on the taps and set a boiler on top of a fifty-five gallon drum not far from the spot where we'd had our pig-raising (and slaughtering) experience. It was a good sap run that winter, and we were kept pretty busy feeding the fire in the drum and carrying the buckets and emptying them into the boiler. Then, when Steve and I got home from work, we'd boil into the night

At the time we had a home-helper—part of an employment program at the Belchertown State School. Anita came to clean the house several days a week, and her supervisor dropped her off. Anita's housekeeping skills left quite a bit to be desired, but when it came to sap collecting, she was a crackerjack. She loved collecting the sap buckets and emptying them into the boiler, so mostly that's what she did. She was good at that.

After the sap season, Anita sort of drifted off and the house, somehow, seemed cleaner.

Steve

Maple sugaring has a long learning curve. It seems that every sap season, we're learning something new—trying to master a new technique or learning to run a new piece of equipment— and while we've gotten increasingly productive and much better informed, we're still on that curve and a lot of what we learn is through trial and error.

When I say "we", I mean me and Meg, but in the business of sugaring, "we" includes our son-in-law Dave O'Brien. I love Dave. I love him, even though we are poles apart in work style and often in outlook. You should also understand that Dave and our daughter Abby own some back land that abuts our orchard, so a joint arrangement in maple sugaring makes sense. I couldn't handle the syrup making without Dave, and he couldn't do it without me.

Well, when we moved up the hill to Orchard House, our sugaring operation kicked into higher gear. I poured a cement pad and bought a second-hand evaporator. This was a step up from the fifty-five gallon drum under the ash tree, and at the time, we thought we were pretty professional. We rigged up a makeshift roof out of a blue tarp to keep us dry while we boiled. It didn't do much to keep out the weather, and boiling could be a pretty miserable experience, so we decided to build a real sugarhouse.

Around these parts, when you're thinking about something new, the first thing you do is ask around to find out what other local people are doing. I found out that most of them built on telephone pole bases so they wouldn't have to pay taxes. Just laid the poles on their sides as a sort of foundation. Well, Dave had some telephone poles because he'd briefly thought of building a barn, except he was going to set the poles vertically. I'd helped him out by digging four or five holes with my Bobcat, and I got poles sunk in those holes. Then Dave decided not to build the barn, and the poles are still standing upright to this day.

Dave's land was practically solid with maple trees, so we built the sugarhouse close to his half-acre and on the orchard's western edge. The sugarhouse, built on those telephone poles, was about fourteen feet by sixteen feet, and we sided it with some rough-sawn pine that our friend Steve McCafferty donated to the project. With a cement pad and a metal roof, we opened our sugarhouse for business.

Turns out that a sugarhouse is like a sailboat. There's always a bigger one out there in the future—bigger and better.

We used that first sugarhouse one season and determined it just wasn't large enough to handle our operation. We needed a bigger one.

Now it happened that up in Templeton, there was a state school, a lot like the Belchertown State School, and they'd had a sugarhouse and all the equipment. And they wanted to sell it all. So Dave and I went up to Templeton, and we met with two old guys who'd been running the operation. I say old, but who'm I kidding? They were around my age.

The place was huge. And they had every piece of equipment a sugaring operation would ever need and all of it was in mint condition. Rubber mats to stand on, scoops, pans, overhead racks, 400 sap buckets, a cap for the stack, and an evaporator that was 12 feet long plus a front pan that was 3-foot by 3. Well, that simply wasn't going to fit in our sugarhouse. Not even close.

So the old guys were explaining why they were getting out of the sugaring business—the maple trees were dying off and getting scarcer, a lot of effort was required, and so forth.

I inquired what they were asking for the whole thing.

"Well," one of the guys said, "we think we can get a thousand dollars."

Suddenly Dave spoke up. "We'll give you fifteen hundred," he said.

I couldn't believe I'd heard him. My head swiveled 90 degrees and I gave him a look. But I didn't say anything until we were back in the car.

"Fifteen hundred bucks? Dave! What were you thinking?"

Well, it had been said and done, so we all shook hands on the deal and we took everything. Even at fifteen hundred, it was a bargain.

The guys were more than helpful. We had to move a shed's worth of wood to get the evaporator out. Meg and I went up and shifted out the wood, and the guys pulled the evaporator out with a Bobcat and put it on our trailer.

The last thing we took was the cap. A cap for a boiler stack keeps out the weather and other things of nature that shouldn't be in syrup, and it is essential equipment. Getting the cap down, however, required a ladder.

"I'm not touchin' it," Dave said. "I hate ladders. Leave it where it is."

Now both of us, as arborists, have gone up more trees in climbing saddles than either of us can count, and I don't like ladders any more than Dave does. However, I'm not one to leave money on the table, so I climbed up the ladder and got the cap.

So here we were with all this equipment, the major part of which we couldn't use.

Well, we took the bricks out of the evaporator and sold it for $2,500. Then we used the money to buy a new evaporator that fit in our sugarhouse. We got a new front pan too and topped things off with the rescued cap, and on the first boil we burned the pan. Brand new pan. One thousand bucks. And we burned it. Well, we didn't ruin it; in fact we're still using it.

In 2004, we built a newer sugarhouse. The reason I know that date is because I had my two grandsons, Ben and Caleb, set their footprints in the fresh cement, and when I forget when we built, I simply go out and look at that pad.

So we were all set, we thought. But we'd thought that before. And with a sugaring operation, you're never all set. Remember, I said it's like a sailboat?

During boiling, it would get so steamy in the sugarhouse that the condensation dripped on us while we worked. Sometimes I felt I might as well be back boiling under the blue tarp. So Dave bought a hood cover for the back pan and that keeps us dry and keeps the sap cleaner.

Meg

We got 400 sap buckets in the Templeton deal, and I stacked them all in back of the sugarhouse and had plans for most of them. However, the guys in the sugaring partnership got to them first and sold them. Then they used the money to purchase a sap-gathering system with gravity-feed tubing, and they explained that buckets were old-fashioned, inefficient and unhealthy.

Bah!

Well, the old soldered buckets probably do have some health issues because of lead, but I was able to cull around 30 buckets that didn't have solder, and I was planning to replace some of the old ones with new stainless steel buckets. However, in this partnership, I didn't get a vote.

Maybe you've seen sugar bushes rigged out with tubing. It is a gravity-feed system that eliminates the need to hang buckets and haul them in to be emptied. The tubing pattern is arranged so the sap runs downhill toward the sugarhouse, but tubing gives sort of a medical look to maples trees, I think. I mean there they are, all those trees, connected to each other by an intravenous network of tubes. It looks more like a hospital ward than a sugar bush.

We went along with the gravity-feed system for several seasons, but after while, that wasn't good enough for Dave. He bought a vacuum system, which he said was even more efficient than gravity-feed, and his selling point was that we would get double the intake of sap. The vacuum system, pulling the sap along to the storage tank, would allow us to produce a quart of syrup per tap. This was a ratio of 40:1. Anyhow, that's what Dave said.

I felt his calculations were flawed, and I pointed out that the vacuum system only allowed us to use one tap per tree, whereas in the old system, a single tree might support up to three taps.

I fooled around with the numbers for a while, trying to prove my point, and that's never good.

Dave got the final word.

"With a vacuum system, syrup making is easier," he said. "And it's more fun."

Steve

I didn't buy Dave's assertion at first. I wasn't sure " fun" was what we were aiming for. Now I buy it. Sugaring *is* fun—or it should be. We'll be out there most nights in syrup season, boiling away, and friends stop over to socialize. Dave's buddies are there most nights, and a fair amount of beer gets passed around. And that's all part of the fun.

Meg and I do most of the collecting, and Dave and his crew do most of the boiling. By nighttime, when the boiling starts, I'm tired out and more than willing to call it quits for the day. Besides, sugaring season coincides with pruning season in the orchard. Coincides? Cuts into it, is more accurate. As a result I find myself pruning well into March and I get frustrated.

But getting back to the fun. There seems to be a philosophy around here that you can throw more money at anything and have even more fun. And so we bought the R.O.

A reverse osmosis filter—or R.O.—is our newest "gee-whizz". It pumps the sap under high pressure through a membrane-style filter, and working like a desalinization press, it removes water from the sap and measures the sugar content of the sap we've drawn. Sap straight from the tree is about 1% to 2% sugar, but you can increase the sugar content by running the product through the R.O. as many times as you want, aiming, for example, for a 5% or 6% concentration. The R.O. cuts down the boiling time and also cuts the amount of wood that you're loading and burning.

A six to seven hour traditional boil, for instance, might yield four gallons of syrup. The R.O. could take 300 gallons of sap and produce 150 gallons of concentrate in roughly two hours. Significantly higher production in less than half the time.

Derek is the guy at our local package store. When he heard about the R.O. he remarked, "Cuts the boiling time, eh? It's also cutting down on the beer consumption and therefore cutting into my sales. I'm not happy about that."

Meg

From the R.O., the sap goes to the evaporator—that's the big stainless steel box that sits on a firebox—the thing we keep building new sugarhouses to hold. We push wood into the firebox continually and boil like mad to reduce the water in the sap. When it gets to a 67% sugar content, we've got maple syrup.

Now the new syrup goes to a filter press to remove the fine particles that are simply the nutrients from the trees that haven't yet dissolved. They aren't harmful—and removing them is just cosmetic—but we want clear syrup

Finishing is the last step in the syrup-making process. I'm in charge of finishing—that means bottling. For a while we were bottling in a corner of the sugarhouse with boiling and fire-stoking going on right at my elbow. But we really needed a clean room. Not one in the industrial sense, as if we were making semiconductors or something, but someplace—a separate area—away from the boiling process. And so I went online, and I found just what I wanted! Someone was selling a former ice cream shack. And it was listed for $2,000.

Well, Steve talked the owner down to $1,200, and he remarked that it was a good thing he'd done the talking instead of Dave or the shack would have cost $2,500.

We had to move the shack to our property, of course, but Steve knew someone who moves sheds and who was willing to do the job for $300.

We set our $1,500 bottling room on 4x4's, laid down a linoleum floor and I was all set!

The syrup has to be heated at least to 180 degrees F before it's poured into sterile containers and sealed. For a long while we were buying plastic syrup jugs—the ones with the maple leaves and snow scenes screened on the sides—and we'd paste on our Sentinel Farm labels. But then there was a plastic syrup jug shortage, and I started bottling our syrup in canning jars. I like the jars. You can see the color of the syrup (syrup is graded by color), and you can also see exactly how much syrup you have left in your jar. Jars of maple syrup standing all in a row in the sunshine is a beautiful sight. Delicious.

Steve

The maple syrup season lasts roughly seven weeks. This past season we realized about sixty gallons of syrup, and we sell it for $24 a quart. In terms of profit, put it this way: we don't lose money. We're able to pay off the equipment and make a little besides. Furthermore, the money from syrup sales helps the farm's cash flow, tiding us over until fall when the apple season starts.

As I said, I'm starting to agree with Dave. We do this because it's fun.

And that other thing I said earlier about the sailboat...that remark holds too. We're still at it—still improving. Last fall we built a 12 x 14 foot shelter onto the front of the sugarhouse. We said it was to keep the wood dry. But then it seemed like a good idea to string lights around the perimeter—make it sort of festive. Now, when you look back toward the woods on nights when the sugarhouse is lighted, it looks like a lantern glowing back there. It looks like there might be a party in progress. And there often is. It's a sociable place, the sugarhouse. And it also helps out our neighbor Derek. His beer sales are rising again.

CIDER PRESSING

Meg

We're still using the cider press we built from a kit sold by the Jaffrey Cider Press Company. Steve put it together back in the 'sixties when we were living on Bay Road. We bought the press even though we didn't own an apple orchard or a crystal ball to let us see that someday we would. We'd sort of sneak over to Atkins Farm orchard and pick up drops. We certainly never took fruit from the trees, but we'd grub along under the trees and harvest a haul of drops, and carry them home to our cider press.

The press concept is pretty simple. You select your apples, wash them well and grind them. The ground apples go into the press's hopper, and you dial down the pressing screw, and keep turning, and all the juice that's in the fruit drains down out of the tub into whatever receptacle you've provided.

The cider press came with a hand grinder, but we found that grinding was long and tiresome work, so Steve connected an electric motor. We're still using that original kit model, and very happily too.

Steve

Our cider pressing kicked into a higher gear after we established Sentinel Farm We became more concerned with cleanliness, since we weren't just pressing a few apples for ourselves and doing it just for the fun of it.

Looking to make our pressing more hygienic, I decided a stainless steel chamber would be ideal, but we had to have one fabricated. I went to a local outfit and started working with an old guy who worked there.

"Tell me what you want," he said.

And when I explained, he got very animated. I guess our cider press was more interesting than the HVAC stuff he normally worked with.

"Yeah," he said—he was all enthusiastic—"we'll put on a spout. I can figure that out and do it for you."

Anyhow, now we have this slick chamber, and Meg, the Queen of Clorox, is always very concerned with cleanliness and she keeps it whistle-clean.

We aren't really allowed to sell our cider. Cider is considered a potentially hazardous food substance. If we were to sell it, we'd have to put on labels that say something like "this is potentially hazardous and can cause any number of terrible things to happen, including death."

Meg

Our cider is unpasteurized. I think that's why we aren't supposed to sell it. I tried a blind taste testing once. I pasteurized some cider—which is very easy to do. All you do is boil it. And I put out the pasteurized and unpasteurized cider side by side. Every single taster voted for the unpasteurized version.

Steve

We do sell a little cider, but only to people we know and trust. I give the same advice to would-be cider buyers that I give to people who shop at the farmers' markets. "Know your farmer," I say. "Visit the farm. Look around and ask questions. Then make your own decision whether this is a farmer you would buy from—someone you would trust with your food."

Meg

Although we don't sell cider to the general public, we do offer a Press-UR-Own operation during Pick-UR-Own. This is a tremendously popular family activity, and I suppose it could be a profit center too, although a very small enterprise.

We set up the cider press along with a barrel of apples and a wash station complete with vegetable brushes. Guests select whatever apples they want—there's a reject pile for the fruit that doesn't make the grade. (The rejects get recycled into our Slingshot Game.) We teach them how to use the equipment—the grinder and press and bottling equipment. And we explain that yes, the whole apple goes into the grinder, core, stem and all. Then the customers wash the apples they've selected and put them into the grinder and press away; next we show them how to bottle their cider. This way, they've made their own cider and are therefore responsible for what they've made.

Our grandson Caleb is a competent cider maker and an excellent instructor. When he's around he is in charge of Press-UR-Own.

Steve

We get some very anal people at the cider press. We allow about one hour per group—that's plenty of time to choose apples, wash and press them. But some folks take forever to inspect and choose their apples. Any little speck or discoloration and they think the apple should fail.

One fall afternoon, a family was out there for the longest time. After more than two hours had passed, and it was starting to get dark, I had to go out and explain that it was way past closing time.

"Time's up," I had to say. "Bottle your cider and be on your way."

Meg

When Abby was in kindergarten, we offered to host a cider pressing just for her classmates. The teacher and the whole class walked down from the elementary school, and we showed them how the press worked. And of course we let them try it themselves. Well, in no time they were gathering apples and dropping them and chattering, and a few were throwing them at classmates when they thought they could get away with it. The kids were working the press and drinking the cider, and the yellow jackets, attracted by the sweet cider and the apple mash, were flying all around. It was a great success. A sticky, messy, exhausting, enormous success.

And every year after that first field trip, teachers have brought classes down to Sentinel Farm for an afternoon of cider pressing. My mother would get into it—serving up cider and wiping noses and chins—and Molly, our younger daughter, loved it. Long after her own kindergarten days, she'd take an afternoon off from high school to direct the cider pressing operation and get in on the fun.

The event ended a few years ago though. The teachers didn't want to walk all the way down from the elementary school. They thought a bus would be better idea, but the school committee wouldn't go for it.

That was fine with Steve and me. We aren't getting any younger.

Steve

Now when you have a cider pressing operation, the subject of hard cider always comes up. I get requests for it every year.

I've been experimenting with hard cider for several years, and some of the results I've produced in the learning process have been...well, I'll just say interesting.

I've tried three times to produce a product I'm happy with, and I've been disappointed with the results each time. I've tasted and tried all sorts of other people's cider, and I've even taken a couple hard cider workshops.

Finally I talked with another beekeeper/orchardist who makes hard cider, and I tasted his product.

"What'd ya think"?" he asked.

I looked him in the eye.

"The stuff's no damn good," I said.

He grinned. "You know, I agree with you."

So I've finally concluded that I just don't like hard cider. And I've stopped trying to make it. My heart's not in it. And if I ever get a taste for hard cider, I'll go and buy some.

Meg

I always like to see how I can use whatever we produce here at Sentinel Farm, and cider is no exception. There's a craze now for apple cider vinegar—it's in all the health stores. To make it, you need a *mother*, which is simply a colony of beneficial bacteria that occurs naturally in unpasteurized and unfiltered apple cider vinegar. I make sure that at least some of the *mother* gets into each bottle of vinegar that has the Sentinel Farm label. The vinegar is slightly cloudy and you can recognize the *mother* in the sediment. I test pH very carefully, aiming for a 4.2% acidity before I decant it into pretty, sterilized bottles and paste on the label.

You can make a nice salad dressing from boiled vinegar

or you can boil the cider longer and produce a delicious cider jelly. No need to add pectin; the apples themselves have plenty of pectin.

Sentinel Farm apple cider vinegar and cider jelly are packed into every gift basket at Christmastime.

BEEKEEPING

Steve

The bees were originally Meg's project. She was the beekeeper until I took over. Our beekeeping started long before there was a Sentinel Farm. We started keeping bees years ago while we were still living on Bay Road.

Meg

The Lockes lived directly across the road and Larry Locke's father, down in New London, had a hive of bees. Well, he died, and Larry offered me everything—the hive, the bees, the beekeeper's vest, the veil—everything. All I had to do was drive to New London and get it.

I read a little about beekeeping, but I didn't read much. I did know that you had to have a screen to contain the bees while you transport them.

So I got a screen. It was actually a screen from a playpen I'd built once, and I put the screen in our ancient Opal Cadet and set off by myself for New London, Connecticut. There was no GPS in those days, and I had no idea where I was going, so I can't think how I got there, but I managed.

I hefted the hive—with the bees inside—into the Opal, put the screen on top and started driving home to Belchertown. The bees didn't even notice my screen. They started flying around inside the Opal—and there was a lot of buzzing from the bees and ducking and dodging from me—but I made it home and set the hive up.

Then the bees that were the collectors went about the business of gathering nectar, and they brought it back to the worker bees in the hive who turned it into honey after stuffing it into little wax cells. And things went along very nicely.

I should probably stop right here and explain who's who when it comes to bees. There's the queen, of course. Then there are worker bees (sterile females) who have various jobs— some are collectors, bringing in the pollen, others are nurses for the young, still others handle wax production and cleaning, and some guard the hives against intruders. Finally, there are the drones. These are the male bees, and their only purpose is breeding; they fly out and mate with virgin queens from other bee colonies and they die as soon as they mate. The drones that haven't successfully mated, come back to the hive; but then, when the breeding season ends, they become a drain on the hive's resources, and the worker bees kick them out. Evict them.

Steve

About the time we moved to the Yellow House—we'd taken our hive along with us, of course—I got interested in beekeeping, and I sort of took it over from Meg. Meg would sometimes panic and run along the top of the stonewall where the hive stood. I tended to move more quietly. So I got myself a helmet and our apiary started expanding.

Since Meg explained about bees, maybe I'll talk about the hives. A hive is made up of stacks of bee boxes called supers, each is fitted with ten frames, and each frame is filled with bees making wax cells and producing honey. I always marvel at those eight-sided cells of wax. Each is perfect, uniformly sized, and angled slightly upward, I'd say about 10 degrees, so the wax won't leak out. Every time I pull out a frame, I marvel at its geometry and at the amazing production that is going on right before my eyes. Those phrases "hive of industry" and "busy as bees", well, that perfectly describes what goes on in each frame. Bees are industriously filling cells, storing up food for the cold season when they will eat through the honey stores. Honeybees are the only insects that store food for such long-term use.

The bees "share" their honey with us, but I have to be careful to take no more than about 50% and leave half so the bees can overwinter.

All the wax foundations are attached to frames, ten frames per box, and the boxes, or supers, are stacked to form a hive that sits on a bee stand. There's a bottom board, then the supers are added according to size—largest, medium and shallow.

At the end of the season, when all nine frames in each box are filled and the cells are capped with wax, each box can weigh about fifty pounds. In your old age, this can present a hefty challenge.

Each hive has to have a queen. When my bee order arrives from an outfit in Georgia, the queen is already bred. And once she is established in her new hive, she is ready to start laying eggs. She will lay over 1,000 eggs in 26 days.

There's an art to introducing a queen bee to her new home. She arrives in a special box with a couple attending nurse bees and a supply of sugar candy. You must introduce her to the hive slowly, keeping her warm while you do so, and getting the bees to chew the sugar candy thereby getting them to accept the scent of the queen.

When a hive gets too full, the queen leaves the hive and splits the colony. This is nature's way of reproducing whole colonies of honeybees. As she leaves, the old queen takes with her about half the worker bees and as much honey as those workers can carry. They land in a cluster on something not far away—a branch or a fencepost or a gutter.

Sometimes you'll come across a swarm of wild bees, and that swarm can be collected and you get a whole new colony. That's like finding gold in the street.

Meg

The famous Fournier swarm was on a gutter. I was still new to beekeeping when that event took place.

The Fourniers were our next door neighbors on Bay Road. Well, they lived a-ways down the road and around a curve and over a hill, but there weren't any neighbors between our houses, so technically, they lived next door. We'd see them driving past in their truck.

Anyway, Mrs. Fournier came storming down to see me one day and she was mad. She was known to be kind of a witch, but on that day she was screaming that my bees had escaped and were attacking.

"They're trying to get into my house," she yelled. "Come and get your damn bees off my property!"

I wasn't quick enough to say, "How do you know they're *my* bees? Let's look in my hive and find out."

They could have been wild bees or feral bees or anyone's bees, but I just told Mrs. Fournier that I was very very sorry and I'd be right down to deal with them.

I hurried and got into my bee suit—and since I was about eight months pregnant at the time, that suit was a tight fit.

But I got it fastened—finally—and I got my helmet and I hustled down to Fourniers'.

There was indeed a swarm of bees against the house. They weren't trying to get inside as Mrs. Fournier had claimed, but they were clustered up around a gutter, and it was quite a swarm.

The Fourniers lent me a ladder, which was kind, I suppose, but it would have been kinder if Mr. Fournier had offered to climb it. Since he didn't, I climbed up to the gutter, but I had no idea how to catch a swarm of bees, so I batted at them. Then I sort of swatted the swarm down and the bees flew off in a single cloud. Then I climbed carefully down.

Steve

Bees are extremely docile when they swarm. If there's a swarm on a branch, I generally put a hive box under the swarm. Then, moving very slowly and quietly, I cut the branch and gently shake it over a hive box until the bees fall into the box, and if the queen is among them, what happens is all well. They are very well-mannered. I generally wait until nightfall and put a cover on the box. Then, lo and behold, we have another hive.

I've been stung plenty of times. In fact, I've been stung right through my gloves.

I got to worrying about it some—worrying I'd develop a fatal allergy or something—so I asked my doctor about getting an EpiPen.

"Don't do it!" he said. "You won't know what you're doing. Call 911."

"Well, maybe I should have an EpiPen in case someone comes to Pick-UR-Own and gets stung."

"No, no, no, you don't want to do that!" He was emphatic. "Liability. You don't know what you're doing with an EpiPen, do you?"

Well, I didn't.

I do know a cure for a bee sting though. Stick a penny right on the sting with a piece of Scotch tape; it'll take away the pain and the swelling.

Eventually I took my gloves off while I worked with the bees; the gloves were clumsy and the bees could sting right through them anyhow. And the thing is, I've never been stung once on my bare hands. Not once. As I said, bees are docile, and if you just take it slow and don't accidently drop a frame, you'll be just fine.

Meg

We were still on Bay Road with that first hive, and I was still the novice beekeeper, when it came time to extract the honey. I suppose we could have bought a honey extractor, but that didn't occur to me. Besides, I wanted to build my own extractor. So I got a barrel from someplace—I think someone was using it as a garbage can—but it was a very nice barrel with waxy sides and I scrubbed it out thoroughly. Then I drilled a hole in the barrel's bottom and another hole in the top. I ran a shower curtain rod between the holes and used some marine-grade plywood to cut two triangles—one for the top of the rod and one for the bottom. Three comb frames at a time could hang from the top triangle and a wrapping of hardware cloth prevented the frames from being casualties of centrifugal force and flying off during extracting.

I got the crank off an old bicycle and rigged it at the top of the barrel to spin the extractor, and Steve hooked an electric motor to the crank and it was perfect. Perfect! The thing worked like a charm and the honey spun out, coated the walls of the barrel and dripped down through the hole in the barrel's bottom.

Perfect.

Steve

Just as Meg's chickens are the targets of predators, our beehives are too. Mice love the hives because they are warm—usually around 90 degrees; the bees generate the heat with their wings. Raccoons and skunks love the honey, and so do the bears. One morning I saw that the horses had gotten out and that the gate was broken. When I went out to investigate, I found that the hives had been taken apart and bees were flying everywhere. Hoping the queen was still there, I started putting the hives back together, and that's when I saw the bear scat. Then it all came together. I figure the bear scared the horses and when they caused a commotion and busted down the gate, they scared the bear.

We've never had a bear since that time, although they're around. A big old bear waddled right down Cottage Street last week, and our neighbor down the hill has his garbage can riffled regularly. But bears have good memories. I guess they don't want to take a chance on those horses.

As an orchardist, I think I have a special appreciation for *apis mellifera*, the honeybee. At blossom time I get very anxious if I don't see enough bees working alongside me in the orchard. They are essential for pollination. At the same time, the fruit trees and wildflowers growing on the farm are essential to the bees that depend on pollen for their existence. One hand washes the other. Apple blossom honey is a wonderful thing.

With beekeeping, there's always something to learn, and I enjoy it. In a good year, our small operation can more than pay for itself, and for several months it helps out the cash flow. We get about ten dollars per pound of honey, and between maple syrup season and the time the fruit crop is harvested, honey provides Sentinel Farm with a nice product.

A SUGAR RANT

Steve

Shortly after we wrote "Sweet Stuff", the branch of our government known as the Food and Drug Administration intervened once again under the banner of "consumer protection". The FDA is finishing up a mandate that says producers of maple syrup and honey must add some new language to their labeling. The words "added sugars" are now being proposed for inclusion on those products.

I object. Strenuously. And for all the good it will do—i.e. none—I have told the FDA so.

Maple syrup and honey are *natural* sugars. Not refined. We (the producers) don't add a thing. Mother Nature put in all the sugar that's needed.

If we made new labels for our Sentinel Farm syrup and honey—labels with the language "added sugar"—we'd be in violation of the truth in advertising laws. We'd be lying, because we *don't* add sugar. We *can't* add sugar.

The truth in advertising laws were probably designed to protect the consumer and the FDA's new piece of busy-work, parading under the same banner, directly butts heads with the truth in advertising authors.

What's a humble producer of maple syrup and honey to do?

We are just small farmers trying to produce and sell a wholesome product to local folks. We're trying to make a few bucks while conscientiously providing food that is pure and wholesome. Do consumers have a right to protection? Sure. But they also have a right to truth.

Both syrup and honey already carry nutritional labels indicating grams of sugar and serving sizes. The list of ingredients on syrup labels says "pure" maple syrup. And that's it. There's nothing else. No water. No preservatives. No added sugar. What part of "pure" doesn't the FDA understand?

I'm frustrated, but I'll tell you this: if the opposing branches of the FDA—the "truth in advertising" people and the "added sugar" folks—get into a brawl, I want a seat at ringside. I'd even pay something to see it.

TO MARKET, TO MARKET

Steve

"Well, I'll grow these apples and pick them, and then I'll sell them." I wonder how many would-be farmers start with those words and that dream. Well, here's the reality:

You can't just grow a crop and sell it. That's my message to anyone thinking about farming.

Think about answering these questions:

You want to sell the stuff you raise? Okay. Do you want to sell wholesale or retail? Where are you going to sell? For how much? How are you going to get your crop to market? And where is that market? Who's your competition?

We started selling at farmers' markets in 2005, but long before that, we had a farm stand.

Meg

That was fun. I was growing vegetables—not enough to take to a market, even if we'd thought about it—but enough to put out in an honor-system farm stand in front of the Yellow House.

It was fun because I got to build the stands and each one was a variation on the one before except each one got better and bigger.

The first one was on a trailer bed, and then we built a more permanent-looking stand. And we decorated it with canvas awnings and signage. Oh, we got very fancy.

If you've ever wondered if an honor-system farm stand can be profitable, I'd say yes—moderately profitable—but there are a few things to watch out for.

Pilferage is one. At our stand, the cash and the vegetables weren't coming out even for a while, and we figured out that a neighbor kid was helping himself to the cash box. So Steve built another box out of solid oak. It had a flap-down lid with a slot for the money and a padlock, and Steve screwed the thing to one of the stand supports. Well, that cured pilferage from the cash box, and it taught us to trust but to take precautions.

Shrinkage is pilferage applied to product—in our case, produce. While the public is generally honorable, we're pretty sure a few people swiped some produce as they were passing by. When we put the stand down on East Walnut Street, which is a fairly busy road with a lot of people passing, shrinkage increased noticeably. That stopped when we moved the farm stand back up near the house.

Two-legged visitors aren't the only cause of shrinkage. The local varmints—squirrels mainly—"shop" the stand during off hours. We wouldn't mind so much if they took a summer squash or a peach and ate it, but no. The squirrels take two bites out of one vegetable, then move on to the next. One squirrel can ruin an entire basket of product. They don't pay for the stuff either.

Sometimes the daily crop and the cash don't come out even. Maybe someone didn't have change on a certain day and "bought" the produce anyway, but generally, a couple days later, we'd see we were cash-ahead, so we'd figure the person had stopped by to true-up.

Basically the honor-system farm stand concept works. At least around these parts. I'm not sure you could say the same if you lived in a city.

Steve

We still operate a farm stand of sorts, even though we've graduated to farmers' markets.

We bought a small refrigerator with a glass door so people can look in and see what we've got for sale. We plug it in on the front porch and park the Amish buggy with a sign in front of the house and people stop by for apples or peaches. Also for blueberries, and for the eggs from Meg's hens, of course. We're still on the honor system. We wouldn't sell maple syrup or honey that way, though.

Meg

One of the challenges of running a farm stand, aside from pilferage and shrinkage, is getting people to know it's there and getting them into the habit of stopping by. So we had to learn to stock consistently. You can't have people coming over for blueberries and not finding blueberries. A couple of futile trips, and those folks are lost as customers for good.

Steve

When we started bringing in a good, reliable crop, we decided that we wanted to sell our fruit retail. And that's mainly how we sell now. We do sell some apples wholesale on occasion, and of course we do Pick-UR-Own, but we signed on with several local farmers' markets, and right away Meg and I entered a whole new universe.

Here are some farmers' markets facts of life that we

learned.

A market is only as good as it's vendors. Or as good as the market manager.

Although variety is essential, a single, average-sized market can't support more than one vendor selling a specific product. For example, Sentinel Farm makes both honey and maple syrup, but we don't sell it at the markets we go to because there are already vendors selling honey and maple syrup at those venues.

I was working down at the sugar house one day when this fella I knew—Ed Parker—came stamping down through the snow.

"I'm on the Board of the South Hadley market," he said, "and we need to sign up an apple-peach vendor. It's been a pretty good market for us. Are you interested?"

Now I knew Ed because he produced maple syrup and had some other maple products, but he and I both understood I wouldn't sell my syrup in South Hadley because he was already there. But I told him sure, I'd be their apple-peach vendor, and South Hadley turned out to be a pretty good market for us too. At least for a while.

Well, Ed Parker went to his reward and the market management changed. They got a new director a couple of years ago and suddenly they weren't honoring their exclusivity policy. Two new apple vendors came in, and one of them brought stuff he hadn't even grown himself. He'd bought it wholesale and was selling it at the market. And the other vendor—I don't know whether it was his produce or not—but he was low-balling the price of apples. People who come to famers' markets want—and should expect—to buy locally grown food. When the food at a market is not locally grown, I believe those customers are short-changed.

So this is a warning I'd give customers who shop at

farmers' markets. Pay attention to what you are buying. Don't just assume that the produce you are looking at was grown locally. Some vendors pad out their stock with stuff they purchase at wholesale. And who knows where some of that stuff has come from. Know your vendor. Visit the farm if you can, and as in all things, buyer beware.

Meg

If you see bananas at your local farmers' market, take that as a clue.

Steve

As I said, the South Hadley market worked well for a while, but after the vendor policy changed, we started giving that market a harder look. For one thing, it's a lot of work, loading produce and hauling it to market, and a good market makes the vendor area accessible. Ideally, there should be parking space right by each booth. South Hadley didn't offer very convenient parking. We had to park at a distance and haul the produce in on shank's mare. So we looked at the figures and decided that the declining income from the market wasn't compensating us for the work it took to go there. And then, factoring in the competition from other apple vendors that was undercutting our sales, we decided to quit selling fruit at South Hadley. But since Ed Parker had gone to his reward, we were able to bring in maple syrup; and we do that once a month.

Meg

Another way to judge a farmer's market is to look at the manager. A good manager has good relationships with vendors. And a good manager has to know the make-up of the local population because the customers will be drawn from there. There was a market in the center of Springfield a while back, that had a crackerjack manager. Then she quit. She said the vendors refused to carry the products her customers wanted. She pointed out that this was a diverse neighborhood with several different ethnic groups that wanted to shop at that market, but they just couldn't get the food they wanted there.

Now my idea of a really good market manager is Belle Rita Novak. She's one smart lady.

You either like Belle Rita Novak or you can't stand her, and Belle Rita doesn't care which way you feel. She is totally focused on managing the Farmers' Market at Forest Park in Springfield, Massachusetts, and she's not there to be anyone's sweetie pie. She is efficient, outspoken, occasionally rude and always effective. When you Google area markets, you'll see that The Market at Forest Park always leads the league. It's profitable and popular.

Belle Rita is who you'd like to have managing any market where you are a vendor. Well, you might wish she were a little more polite and refined—but then, she wouldn't be Belle Rita Novak.

People from all over —Asia, South America, Africa—live in the area and meeting their food needs is a challenge that Belle Rita really gets into. She goes out of her way to bring in the foods her customers know and like.

It was stiflingly hot the day Steve and I met Belle Rita and while she talked with us, she was busy stuffing ice cubes down her shirt. Steve made some smart-ass remark, and Belle Rita took an instant like to him. So when she saw us at the New England Vegetable & Fruit Conference recently, she plunked herself into a chair next to me and right away started turning around and giving orders. Belle Rita is someone my grandmother would have described as "sizable". She's loud too, and people take notice.

"Bring me coffee!"

"Shut up and listen ..."

Anyhow, I had elected a lecture called "An Integrated Approach to Growing and Marketing Ethnic Crops"—which of course was right up Belle Rita's alley. She was really keen to learn more about what her market wanted.

Springfield has a large ethnic population, of course, but Belchertown doesn't. Still, I'd like to grow things that people want, and I expect more ethnic peoples of different nationalities will be moving in.

There was a woman from Africa once, who came to the orchard for Pick-UR-Own, and she kept looking at the pigweed instead of the apples. She was thrilled with the pigweed, except she called it callaloo. Pigweed, I thought—well, callaloo—you can't eat *that*. Well, I finally Googled it and found out that callaloo is part of the Amaranth family which includes a leafy vegetable that was probably familiar to her from "home." That pigweed probably looked pretty good to a homesick African finding herself in Belchertown, Massachusetts.

As we sat there, Belle Rita gave me a bit of education about her ethnic customers.

"Did you know," she demanded, "that ethnic peoples homecook twice as much food as Americans do? *Twice* as much! And not only do they cook it..." she leaned into my face... "they BUY it. And where? Where do they buy it? At the markets!"

Leaving me to think about this, Belle Rita turned back to the lecture, having enlisted another ally in her crusade to supply the produce that ethnic people wanted. She got me fired up too. I got some seeds for ethnic vegetables at the New England Vegetable &Fruit Growers Conference, and some of them were free! Johnny's Seeds in Maine is a good supplier of these types of vegetables. I hope that woman from Africa comes back.

Steve

Now I'm going to open a topic under the general heading of "Government."

We participate in several farmers' markets including — logically—the Belchertown Farmers and Artisans Market that is held every Sunday morning in summer on the Common. I am on the board, and it can be a difficult board to serve on, especially as a vendor. It operates under the vague oversight of the AgCom, our town's agricultural commission. Any rural community or one with a good amount of agriculture is supposed to have an AgCom, which is a standing committee whose appointed members are primarily engaged in farming. The members are responsible for: representing the farming community, encouraging the pursuit of agriculture, promoting agricultural-based economic opportunities, and preserving, revitalizing and sustaining the community's agricultural businesses and lands. (I copied that from the website.)

Now there are regulations that govern most farmers' markets, and when I consider them, I'm amazed that the markets function at all.

To set up in a specific farmers' market, the supporting group has to present the town with a certificate of insurance. Fine. But to obtain that certificate, the market has to be a legal entity. So often the would-be market has to get an attorney to go through the rig-a-marole of creating that entity. Then it has to pay the attorney.

Each vendor is required to present the market with their own certificate of insurance, proving that they are properly insured. This could cost as much as $700 or $800.

This eliminates some folks who would simply like to sell something at the market. Take, for instance, the person in Belchertown who wanted to sell the birdhouses she makes out of old shoes. I bought one. It's a tennis shoe with a little roof nailed on. She can't sell enough of those birdhouses to make back the cost of the insurance policy to merit the certificate. So she loses and so do the all the people who'd like to buy birdhouses made out of old shoes.

Some markets require a board of directors. So you have to find people willing to serve on the market's board. Recruiting volunteers for a market board probably isn't any harder than recruiting volunteers anywhere, but I doubt it's any easier. We've had people agree to serve who've had no idea what a committee should do or how it should function. Good folks, to be sure, well-meaning but not well-informed.

You need to hold the market somewhere, and there's a cost to vendors for renting space, of course. Let's say a board offers vendors space that rents for $25/per market. An average market is seventeen weeks, so there goes $425 for rental.

Sometimes a board of health gets into the act. And boards of health differ from town to town; some are fairly lenient and some are unreasonable sticklers. Belchertown is strict. Meg makes dried apples. The board wanted to know exactly how she made them. Did she take out the proper amount of moisture during the drying? Did she weigh the apples before drying and again after to determine this moisture content? The Board of Health admonished one vendor at our market for stripping. No, not clothes, for stripping corn. He was peeling back a small amount of husk so customers could peek at the kernels.

So I'd list all that under "local government procedures and regulations." I'd like to add "interference" to the list, and I haven't even covered the whole topic yet.

Meg

Farmers who bring food to markets have to keep up-to-date on government regulations and on all sorts of other things like plant stock and pests, techniques and tools and so forth. So Steve and I, wanting to be informed and conscientious food producers, subscribe to a number of publications and attend whatever workshops we can. One of the best is The New England Vegetable & Fruit Conference that is held every other year in Manchester, New Hampshire. This is a three-day intensive conference sponsored by the Universities of Maine, Massachusetts, Rhode Island, Vermont and Cornell as well as the Connecticut Agricultural Experiment Station and the Maine Organic Farmers and Gardeners Association. And that's where I recently ran into Belle Rita Novak.

A food producer has to find out who wants to buy from you and what they want to buy. So you study your market. I learned a tremendous amount about ethnic produce when I attended that session and sat next to Belle Rita. Some of it, I even learned from the lecturer.

I learned about presentation. That's huge. Whatever produce you're selling, it has to give the impression of abundance. The display has to appear to be overflowing. Now if you're selling something delicate, like peaches, you can't just create a heap of them, or the fruit on the bottom would bruise. So you may have to use a filler, crumpled paper bags or something to lift the produce and make it look like you've got lots and lots.

And color. That's also important. There's research on what colors people respond to and what colors turn them off. Yellow is a winner. People buy when there is yellow in the display, so we try to use yellow, maybe even in an awning.

One presenter who runs several markets in New York City has been terrifically successful. Of course there are a lot of ethnic communities in the city, and he studies them. He sends people out with paper and pencil to record details of market settings. They write down what people buy and who is doing the buying. It was a very exciting lecture.

But that brings me back again to market managers. That job description is much broader than it may first appear—press and promotion, for example. Social media is terrifically important. A market needs a newsletter and a vibrant online presence. And market news has to go out in a timely fashion—at least a week earlier so customers can plan. And the market manager generally has to handle those tasks or has to oversee someone else who will do it.

A market manager needs to enforce the rules. And while he or she needs to respect the vendors and work with them—meeting their needs and listening to them—at the same time they need to listen to the customers and respect and work with them. And they should be doing development as well; that is, getting out into the community and prospecting.

A good market probably has twelve or fifteen vendors minimum. Like a food display, a market has to be large enough to project the sense of abundance. Overflowing bounty—that needs to be the impression.

Steve

Meg and I have found, as farmers, that there's always something new coming along. Farming goes way beyond putting seeds in the ground and picking produce. So as Meg said, we attend the NEVF conferences, and we participate in local seminars and workshops. We read constantly. There's always something new to learn, and we feel we have to be willing to learn. We want to be open to new things. And that includes keeping up with the regulations and programs that the government always seems to be coming up with. There are more than a few farmers who'd like to say, "oh just let me grow my crops, don't bother me with new things." Nevertheless, those new things won't go away.

For a long time, we've participated in state-certified nutritional programs and have accepted WIC and elderly assistance coupons worth $2.50 each. It's a bit of a rig-a-marole, collecting the coupons and stamping them, then sending them away to the government office and waiting for reimbursement. But we look at the people who are using those programs, and most seem careful and grateful.

One time, though, I mailed in the coupons and the post office lost them. An envelope came one day with about half the coupons inside, all torn and dog-eared, along with the post office's boilerplate apology. I had a few words with the local postmaster who told me I should have insured the mailing.

"You told me I *couldn't*," I countered. "I asked, and that's what you told me!"

He sort of huffed and stammered and said that he'd see what he could do. But before he could "see", the rest of the coupons—or most of them—showed up.

One of the government's newest programs is HIP (Healthy Incentive Program) that is attached to SNAP (Supplemental Nutrition Assistance Program) to help low-income individuals and families. Nutritional assistance has gone high tech. Each person (or family) in the program gets an EBT card that they can swipe at a store or market for a value that is determined by their income.

How easy is that?

Easy for the card-holder maybe, but the merchant needs to have a dedicated iPad with an EBT reader and a Bluetooth printer.

I started filling out the application to be a SNAP/HIP retailer, and was about three pages into thing, when our Social

Security numbers were requested.

"Nope," I said, "Not doing this."

And I gave up.

The SNAP people were persistent though, and finally a lady from the local group lulled us into letting her come out and help me enroll.

She showed up at 7:00 AM, right when she said she would, and she brought donuts. Then she went out to the barn with Meg and helped milk the goats. Then she sat down and walked me through the steps of the licensing process and gave me a snazzy iPad, in a sexy case that also contains the reader and the Bluetooth printer. Now I am a SNAP retailer.

Nice. But I know several farmers who have looked at SNAP and said. "Uh-uh, too much trouble. This is where I get off the bus."

But you know, I think it's worth it. With SNAP, I'm making sales I might not otherwise have made. And we can use SNAP down in the apple barn too, because folks are requesting it during Pick-UR-Own. There are some abuses, sure, but Meg and I believe that everyone should have a crack at getting the best food possible.

There are rewards in farming, but remember my warning: You can't just grow your stuff and sell it. There's a lot more to it... and it's not that easy.

PICK-UR-OWN

Steve

We opened the Pick-UR-Own operation shortly after we began selling at famers' markets, and we started it because we wanted to depend less on the markets. By opening the Sentinel Farm orchards to the public, we figured we could offer some of Meg's produce along with the apples, as well as some delicate fruit like peaches that can't stand up to the tough handling of market customers.

There are would-be customers who think you have to squeeze a piece of fruit before you buy it. I don't know why. Squeezing just bruises the fruit and makes it unsalable. I stand there wincing when some ham-handed person is rummaging through a display of pears, for example, squeezing and tossing most aside. I actually smacked some guy's hand one time. Big guy. Hands like catchers' mitts and just about as delicate. His wife laughed.

Apart from avoiding fruit abusers, we figured there'd be other benefits to Pick-UR-Own. We wouldn't have to leave home or haul produce to market, for example. Those would be great time-savers.

Anyhow we put out the Pick-UR-Own signs in time for a Labor Day opening, and from then through Columbus Day we don't accept any weekend social engagements. On Saturdays and Sundays, we are in the orchard practically fulltime.

Now ours is an old orchard. The trees weren't planted in blocks, so the varieties are scattered; there can be a Honey Crisp tree next to a Gravenstein, for example, and the varieties ripen at different times. Gravenstein is an early apple and Honey Crisp comes along much later in the fall. So the customers need some guidance about which trees are ripe for picking, and we try to help them understand that some apples that look ripe actually aren't.

Before every weekend opening, we mark the trees that have fruit ready to be picked. Each one of those trees has a yellow ribbon. I tie a yellow ribbon to a wooden clothespin, write the name of the variety on the pin then pin it to the tree.

Simple, huh? Do you think you could follow that plain instruction? Well, I can tell you that many folks apparently can't.

To make it even clearer, I put out a blackboard listing the varieties of apple that are available each day and explaining again about the yellow ribbons.

"It's not yellow?" the sign says, "Then it's not ripe!"

One day a car with New York plates pulled up and an older woman got out with her daughter. The woman was interested in drops. These are apples that have fallen from the trees and quite a lot of people buy them for applesauce and so forth, and we sell them at the bargain price of fifty-cents a pound. I tell pickers to make sure the skins are not punctured and caution them to wash the apples carefully.

Well, this woman took several bags, went into the orchard

and set to work under the trees.

Her daughter watched for a while, then decided she'd like to pick. No, she didn't want drops; she wanted to pick from the trees. Fine. I gave her a bag and explained about yellow ribbons.

When the younger woman came back, her transparent bag was full of apples that were what I'd call contraband. I saw Sun Crisps, in there and Honey Crisps. In fact every apple she'd picked came from a non-yellow-ribbon tree.

I was irritated.

"What didn't you understand?" I demanded, pointing to the evidence.

She came right back at me.

"Well, at least you don't have to pick these! I did the work for you!"

"No, you didn't. I can't use these apples. They aren't ripe! Every single one has gone to waste."

Then I told her I didn't want to see her on the farm again.

Well, her mother came in with her bags of drops and paid for them and they went on their way. But I was steamed about it. I still am.

Meg

The Pick-UR-Own operation is based in our apple barn, and it gives us the chance to sell products there that we don't take to farmers' markets. Produce like my sweet potatoes, for example. I really don't grow enough to haul to market but they move very nicely in the apple barn. The pears and plums are mostly past by Labor Day, but we usually have some peaches in the cooler and those are for sale. And we offer products that we can't sell in markets because of non-compete rules—products like maple syrup and honey. Those are good sellers in the apple barn. I also sell my goat milk soaps and dried apple rings.

Steve

People always ask how we price our Pick-UR-Own product. We arrived at our prices through trial and error.

When we opened Pick-UR-Own we charged on a per-bag basis. Ten dollars a bag. That lasted exactly one season before we wised up.

We used to give each picker a bag with handles to hold what they'd picked. You should have seen what came up from the orchard to the barn! Handles ripped off the bags from the weight of the apples crammed inside. People waddling along, leaning backwards to balance all the apples overflowing the bags and piled up against chests. Pockets bulging. People still chewing from the half-dozen apples they'd eaten while picking.

So we learned our lesson, and now we charge by the pound. A dollar-fifty per pound.

A long time ago, Art Linkletter got it right when he said: "People are funny."

And here's another "people are funny" tidbit. When we tell them what we charge, some folks say: "Wow. That's a great deal." Others say: "Whoa. So much? I could get apples at Stop and Shop for ninety-nine cents a pound."

Yeah, I think, but where did those apples come from? And how long ago were they picked? I'm tempted to say: "Well, Stop and Shop's still there. You got your choice."

Having said this about pricing, I will also say that we have a sliding scale. If someone wants a bag or two of apples, it's a dollar-fifty-a-pound, but if a customer wants apples by the bushel for baking or making applesauce, well, that's different. We may charge half our regular rate.

Pickers bring their "crop" into the apple barn to be weighed and paid. Now I've been at this so long I can pretty well judge what the weights are going to be, but I've learned—when it's a family with kids—to make a game out of it. There's a little added value in entertainment.

"How much do you think this weighs?" I'll ask one of the kids.

"I dunno. Five pounds?"

"You, Mom, what do you think?"

Parents get right into the game.

"Oh...fifteen pounds?"

I know that the bag is usually around nine pounds and I often tip-off the kid. So the kids are usually the winners in this game, and the prize is a CISA sticker (CISA sends me bunches of them, for some reason). I have learned to hand the sticker to the kid; I don't apply it myself. Not in this day and age.

Now farmers' market pricing is different. At a market, a basket of apples is usually forty dollars a bushel. Honey Crisps, however, are very much in demand right now, and I can get eighty-to-ninety dollars a bushel at the markets.

That's one of the reasons we continue to haul our product to farmers' markets, even though we're running Pick-UR-Own.

Meg

A couple seasons ago our daughter Molly (who is the apple that didn't fall far from the family tree), told us that we needed to "step up our game."

Well, I like to invent things out of other things, and I like to see what I can recycle, and Molly is right there too. According to Molly, we needed a hay slide for the kids. I researched hay slides and found that they involve a huge mound of hay with a slick surface placed on it—a shoot sort of thing—that kids can slide down.

We don't have a hay mound, but we do have a hill that runs down to the apple barn, and I saw how it could make a dandy slide. So after a good bit of research, I acquired some vinyl sheets—the ones used for soffits. I got three sheets, 18-

inches x 12-feet, turned them underside up and laid them end-to-end on the hillside to make a 36-foot run. With help from our grandson Isaac, I braced the sheets on both sides with bales of hay. Then I sprayed the vinyl with silicone and laid in a good supply of burlap sacks that I bought at Amherst Farmers' Supply.

The hay slide is wildly popular. I spray it every day with silicone, and the kids climb into the sacks and whizz down. And not only the kids! The parents can't wait to climb into the burlap sacks too. And they like to do tricks, the parents. They snowboard down the slide standing up. Grandmothers are out there, throwing their arms up in the air and yelling "Whee-eeee!" like they're on a roller coaster.

Molly was right about the hay slide, so we went on to make other Pick-UR-Own amusements.

The Rotten Apple Slingshot is another hit.

Now one of the many things I like about the Rotten Apple Slingshot, other than it's a lot of fun, is that it's made out of material that has been recycled multiple times.

First I'll explain the object of the game. We created a giant slingshot at the edge of a little gully. The target is across the gully about fifty feet away. You step up, load the slingshot with a rotten apple and pull backward...backward...backward, and when you release, the apple hurls toward the target. Well, it does if you aim correctly.

I bought the slingshot itself online. You can get one too. Look under Balloon Launcher. The ends of our slingshot are held by 2x4s screwed to a base that has seen four generations of use in other applications. Originally the base served as packing material for the evaporator we bought. Then we used it as an observation platform so kids visiting the sugarhouse could stand on it and look into the evaporator. When we installed the hood, there wasn't room for the observation platform so we declared it obsolete, moved it outside and used it for storing the old sap buckets that came along in the Templeton deal. And now it's the base, or platform, for the slingshot game. You step up onto the platform, put down your bucket of rotten apples, take the slingshot and walk backwards—pulling—to the back edge of the platform and let fly.

The target for the game is another recycled invention. Originally it was a 500-gallon sap tank that had a wooden frame. We stood it up on end across the gully, about fifty feet from the slingshot, with its bottom-side foremost, and I painted an apple tree on it for the target. When a flying apple hits the target, the metal makes a deep, hollow boom. Very satisfying. Then I got fancy. I fashioned leaves out of aluminum around the edges of the target and when apples hit those, there's a shimmering, rattling noise. It's a game with sound effects.

A basket of rotten apples—which have been recycled from the Press-UR-Own tent—costs $3.00. A blackboard beside the game allows players to write their names and point totals to keep score.

Eleven-year-old Eli is the Rotten Apple champion.

Molly and I made a Ride-the-Horse attraction out of a fifty-five gallon white plastic drum that I got free from a make-your-own beer brewery in Manchester, New Hampshire. I was so excited to get this free drum that I drove to Manchester in the very worst possible snowstorm to get it. Well, I didn't want the brewery people to change their minds about the price of the thing.

I put my good English saddle on the barrel, and we used my mother's old quad cane for the horse's neck and head. We jammed the quad end into the barrel, wrapped the "neck" in hay, then in chicken wire, and fashioned the cane's hook end into the horse's nose. Then we wrapped it up in fabric. The tricky part was hanging the horse. We wanted slings on the front end and back so the rider would have the rocking sense of cantering along. That's where Molly's daughter Sadie got involved as "rider" while Molly and I fussed and adjusted and finally got it working.

I shouldn't forget Press-UR-Own. When we set up the cider pressing activity a few years ago, we quickly found we had a real attraction. It is an active family operation, and as Steve points out, a nice little profit center.

We made a corn hole game—except with apple designs— and we put up a tent with picnic tables underneath.

And finally, we have the goats. Visitors to the orchard are amused and charmed by the goats, especially by the kids— and I try to breed so there are baby goats dancing around at picking time. They rear up on their hind legs and charge at each other in mock battles, and the visitors think that's great.

I think we did a good job of stepping up our game at Pick-UR-Own, just as Molly had suggested.

Steve

We use an electric golf cart in the orchard every day, and it comes in handy at Pick-UR-Own when families happen to bring senior members along. Instead of just sitting at a picnic table watching the show, these folks are welcome to take the key to the cart and ride through the orchard.

I used to park the cart next to the apple barn and leave the key right in the ignition until one afternoon when I looked out into the orchard and saw the cart zooming this way and that like someone had blown up a balloon and let it loose. A kid— a *little* kid—was driving the thing.

"Somebody get that rug rat," I hollered.

And the kid's father took off at a dead run. He didn't seem offended that I'd called his son a rug rat.

Now I keep the key in my pocket.

Meg

We get customers who come back year after year. My favorite customers were members of a Polish family. The wife would arrive looking like she was going shopping at Saks Fifth Avenue. All dolled up, she was. But she was serious about apples, and her family would go through the orchard, picking like mad; then, the very next week when they came again, she'd bring us beautiful pastries that she had made with the apples.

Once a year, her parents would visit from Poland where the father was a farmer. Steve sat down with him at a picnic table one time, and they had quite a conversation. Steve doesn't know a word of Polish and the father had almost no English, but they managed to communicate. The farmer from Poland was interested in the varieties of apple we grow, so Steve held them up one by one and told him what each was. The Polish guy would nod and say something back. They had quite a conversation.

Steve

When we look at the economics of Pick-UR-Own, we can see that profits have picked up steadily each year. And to an extent, the operation has meant we can be selective about the farmers' markets we attend. We can choose the ones that are located close by and that are run in a manner we like.

But to get back to what I said at the start of this chapter—the reason we started Pick-UR-Own was to ease dependency on farmers' markets; but in truth that hasn't happened. The operation has made us less dependent on the markets but it hasn't supplanted them. We still need to go to farmer's markets in order to fully move the produce we grow.

Meg

We are always interested in how people hear about Sentinel Farm. Some people go online to sites like CISA to find listings of Pick-UR-Own operations that are local and sound right for their families. The parents of UMass students are great customers. We put signs out on 202 by the turn-off toward the university, and just before Labor Day we put a big sign on the Belchertown Common. The parents must figure that as long as they're out here dropping off the kids, they might as well get some benefit for themselves, and in they come. Sentinel Farm has a website, and Facebook does a super job of bringing in customers. Then, of course, there's word of mouth—that's powerful.

Steve

We have plenty of Pick-UR-Own competition around these parts, but I remember asking a couple why they came to Sentinel Farm to pick instead of going to one of the huge orchards in the area.

"Because Sentinel Farm isn't commercial," was the answer. "You are local, and we are assured of having a good experience here."

KEEPING UP TO DATE AND WELL-INFORMED

Steve

On a stiflingly hot June day not long ago, I went to an event over in Amherst where there was going to be a number of presentations, demonstrations and exhibits on farm topics. I try to keep well-informed on current practices and new techniques, so I rode over.

Meg, for some reason, had insisted I ride my bike to Amherst, and I, for some reason, went along with it. It had been a long bike ride and I was hot and probably slightly dehydrated, and that might be why I decided to attend the beekeeping lecture. My choice was mostly based on the temperature. The bee tent was under some shade trees and that's where I ended up because at that point, shade was a bigger attraction than beekeeping.

So there I was, sitting on a folding chair near the front—near a hive, actually—when an aggressive bee flew out of the hive, circled my head, and stung me on the nose. It really hurt! A bee sting is bad enough but when it's on your nose, well, that's a sensitive area. My eyes watered. Instantly, I could feel my nose swelling.

So I got up and made for the back of the tent where I could explore my nose in a place less public. It was hot. I was feeling sort of faint, but I stood there, tenderly feeling my nose and wondering how big and red it was becoming. I have this bee sting treatment that I recommend—I described it in the beekeeping chapter—where you tape a penny on the sting. I had a passing vision of myself with a nose like Pinocchio and a copper penny taped to it, and I thought, no, I'm not doing *that*.

So there I stood, hot, faint, in pain and realizing, on top of everything else that was wrong with me, that I was also very vain.

Then all of a sudden the guy presenting the beekeeping lecture yelled, "*Ow!*"

And he slapped *his* nose.

"I've got a stinger in my nose!" he cried.

And he was sort of feeling around on his nose because, you know, if you have a stinger hanging out of your nose it could be kind of embarrassing.

Anyhow, I left the event early. I still had to ride back to Belchertown, and I was a little concerned about the trip. I mean, I was verging on heatstroke and I had a snoot full of venom on board and my sense of balance was pretty far out-of-kilter. I thought about calling Meg, but I decided to tough it out. I just got my bike—it was Meg's bike actually—got it out from behind the Porta-potties, glanced at the ambulance that was parked back there, thought about *that* for a few seconds, then climbed aboard the bike and headed slowly home.

I didn't learn much about beekeeping. Oh, maybe two things: when you attend a beekeeping demonstration, don't sit near the front. And don't ride your wife's bike.

HOW MANY CARBURATORS ON THE FARM?

Steve

The other day my brother-in-law mentioned he'd had the carburetor on his lawn mower cleaned, and it had cost him a hundred and ten bucks. He admitted he got ripped off, but I was staggered. If I had to clean all the working carburetors around this place—and pay that rate—well, I'll tell you this: I don't have that kind of money.

But it did start me wondering: how many carburetors do we actually own? I started counting up the farm equipment, some of which have carburetors, and even before I lost count, the inventory was pretty impressive.

We have a Massey Ferguson tractor

A rototiller

A Ferris 62-inch front deck mower

An electric golf cart for zipping around the orchard, and it sure beats walking miles in a single day.

A Transit Connect van with snazzy signage advertising Sentinel Farm in four colors. Its low back deck allows us to shift produce in and out easily at markets.

Meg

And I can load a whole herd of dwarf goats into the Connect. I've taken them up to the Lake House in New Hampshire a couple of times because I wanted the goats to eat the weeds along the water's edge. That's a trip in more ways than one.

Steve

We have a splitter
 A backhoe
 Two chain saws
 A weed trimmer
 We have a sprayer for the orchard
 A cooler in the apple barn
 A disc harrow
 A cultivator
 A bush hog

Meg

And don't forget the sugarhouse. There's the evaporator in there and a finishing pan and all kinds of ancillary equipment like thermostats and valves.

About the only piece of equipment that works by hand is the cider press. The old cider press that we built back on Bay Road.

Steve

As I started mentally inventorying the equipment around the place, I ran into an issue that's pretty common around the farm—the issue of scarcity. In other words, with all the equipment we *do* have, apparently, we don't have enough.

"Gosh!" I said to myself, "I only have one tractor and one

sprayer. If one or the other of those vital pieces of equipment goes west, I'm dead in the water."

For instance, a couple of weeks ago I got up at 5:00AM because I like to spray early when the wind is calm. I was just getting started when the hose on the sprayer failed. And that was it. By the time I got the problem fixed, I'd missed a critical spray. As a result, I'm seeing more apple scab and I think I spotted some European Apple Sawfly.

Meg

The guy at the tractor supply place—and Steve is there often—calls Steve "the orchard mechanic."

Steve

Well, I am forced to face a number of issues concerning the equipment around this place. Those issues are mostly self-inflicted. Maybe I've put something on backward or assembled it in the wrong order. Most of the time I can figure out the problem and fix it, although it takes up a lot of my time.

Meg

Steve doesn't mind asking people for help either. He isn't afraid to admit, openly and honestly, that he's made a mistake.

Steve

There's a price to pay for that. I ask and I get valuable information because I'm willing to listen. But then the advisor generally goes on—and sometimes on and on—to talk about something else, and I have to stand there and politely listen. You can't just accept advice, you know, and get out Scot-free. Nothing's free.

HAVE WE A MADE A PROFIT YET?

Steve

Well, we didn't really have any grandiose plans when we retired and started this thing—back when we named the place Sentinel Farm and established it as an LLC. Here we were, new to retirement, and I think we were just looking for a venture that would offer some educational opportunities and some interesting challenges. Both Meg and I like to research new things and figure out new ways to get things done. And mindful of Uncle Sam and the state, we wanted to do this legally. What we hoped to do was pay back our expenses and make a little money besides.

To me, this has been a homerun. We've done that.

But profit? The answer depends on what you consider profit. How you define it. Are we each paid a wage? Well, no. Fortunately we have other resources for that. But when we're discussing profit, we'd probably factor in a few intangibles like the satisfaction of producing a wholesome product that people want to buy. A good product that keeps people fed. We'd add in the satisfaction of learning new things and meeting new challenges. And meanwhile, the farm earns enough to pay its bills and buy the equipment it needs. Those are all part of our definition of profit.

To us, profit is the satisfaction we get out of the endeavor.

When we started, we didn't have a business plan other than one in our heads. Our goals were pretty simple. Meet expenses with a bit extra. Produce a good product. Learn new things. Work outdoors.

Meg

If we had written down a formal business plan, we probably wouldn't have become farmers. Sentinel Farm might never have been if we'd planned it by the textbooks. But I had this friend years ago—Sue Thurlow—and I learned an amazing lesson from her.

Sue Thurlow became a single mom on the morning her second baby was born. On that morning her husband decided he didn't want to be a husband or a father, and as they said in the cowboy movies I used to watch, "He lit out."

Well, there she was, Sue Thurlow. Two tiny children, no husband, no job. It was all on her shoulders. This happened during the Great Cheese Period—that time when the government was handing out free blocks of cheese—great big blocks of it—to the elderly and to people on welfare like Sue Thurlow. She raised those kids on macaroni and cheese, and sometimes we took some cheese off her hands to help her out. And this is what she told me:

"I'd start to make a budget, then I'd look at it and realize I wasn't even going to make it as far as tomorrow. So I'd simply close my eyes, put the budget down and go forward and do it anyway."

And she did it. She got herself through college, got herself a job, got a house, raised those two kids and finally found another husband—a better one this time.

Anyhow, I endorse Sue Thurlow's theory of economics. And when we started Sentinel Farm, we followed her example and just went ahead and did it. And it all worked out, just like Sue Thurlow said it would.

We keep careful records of what we've sold and when and where we've sold it. When it comes to economics, Steve handles the books and I handle the taxes. That's our division of labor. At tax time I get a good overview of how we're doing and can see whether we've made a profit.

It's complicated though. Our depreciated farm equipment and farm status are economic factors, and since we are an LLC, the farm can often take a loss that enables our personal tax situation to benefit. As in most things, whether you are aware or not, there is a system at work, and everything is connected to everything else.

Steve

It all has to do with scale. We are a small operation. If we wanted, or expected, the farm to provide one-hundred percent of our support, we'd need to operate on a much larger scale. I'd have to plant differently. Meg would have to pay more attention to value-added products.

But we started this when we retired. And we've seen steady growth, but I'd have to say that the profit we've taken out of Sentinel Farm goes beyond dollars. We're ahead of the game. And we've had a lot of fun.

RETIRING AGAIN

Steve

Meg and I each retired once, and in retirement, we became farmers. Farming is hard work. Easily as hard as the jobs we retired from. It's often worrisome and the monetary rewards can be slim. We were fortunate to have other means of support beyond farming, but this retirement occupation has been consuming and without question, it's become more challenging as we've grown older. Lately, a question has been coming up with increasing frequency. How do we retire from farming? The answer—and we haven't really figured out the answer—is complicated.

Some days, when I think about it, I feel like I'm wearing a big pair of boots and standing in the middle of a huge cow-pie. A great big cow-flap that sucks at my feet. Now when you're in this situation, there are two things you can do. One is to step out of your boots and simply walk away.

We could do that, I suppose. We could hang a for sale sign in front of the house the way Arlan Skinner did. Sell out and walk away. We could simply say: "That's it! We're going to retire for good this time."

Or, when your boots are in deep, you can try to get out of the muck and keep your boots on your feet. Ease out gradually, one foot at a time, holding those boots on with little more than intention and will.

I think we'll probably take the second way and step out slowly. The trouble is, I don't have the balance I once had.

All through this farming process, Meg and I have tried to do due diligence with everything we've undertaken. We've read and studied as much as possible, trying to be informed so as to have a potholder handy before we grabbed a handle. So now, as we move through our eighth decade, we've been seriously looking into this question: how do we retire from farming?

It so happens that there is a local outfit in New England that is ready to help. Land for Good is a non-profit that helps people find and buy both working and open land. It helps folks set up ways to leave their land in trust, and it's also a resource for those who want to sell their farms and for potential buyers who are searching. A representative of Land for Good happens to live near us, and she came over with another rep to conduct a free consult session.

Meg

In thinking about this business of retiring from farming, I have been doing due diligence, as Steve said. I also wrote a few documents about our situation, so I thought we were all ready for the Land for Good consult. They met with us and reviewed my documents. And they would have been happy to work with us, I guess, but when we considered the fees for ongoing consulting—I think it was three-to-four-hundred dollars per consult—Steve and I took a harder look at using

Land for Good to help us out of our cowpie. We decided we'd keep our checkbook closed.

Steve

As the Land for Good folks pointed out, our situation is somewhat unique; its major problem is scale. The operation is too small to support the livelihood of a person who would depend on this farm fulltime for an income. We were hoping to find someone who wanted to come in, work the farm and gradually take over, but finding that person is the issue. And as we considered it, we concluded that the individual—assuming we could find him or her—would really have to live on the property. The rub is, we aren't ready to give up the house.

Meg

One of our grandsons—Caleb—who is presently fifteen, thinks he would like to attend college at UMass's Stockbridge School of Agriculture following in the footsteps of his father and his two grandfathers. Maybe Caleb is a potential person to take over Sentinel Farm. It's nice to think about that, but we really can't count on Caleb to be the next generation to work Sentinel Farm. Nor is it fair to saddle him with our dream as a handy way to give up farming.

Steve

So our retirement from farming is going to happen like the second method of getting out of the cow-pie—the "get-out-slowly-with-your-boots-intact" way. We think we'll probably retire gradually. Rather than taking more profit, we'll look for ways to innovate the farm work taking inspiration, for instance, from the electric pruner we recently bought. It cuts pruning time easily in half and it's fun as well. For the first time, Meg has gotten involved in pruning and she looks forward to using the electric pruner.

We'll also cut back slowly on segments of the farm work. "Retire off" various elements that the farm presently handles. We'll probably give up the farmers' markets and just move what fruit we can with Pick-UR-Own and sales to local people who drop by the apple barn. Retire from the maple sugaring operation. Just turn the whole thing over to Dave O'Brien and simply say, "Your problem now, buddy. Do what you like."

Meg

We'd like to age in place in our farmhouse, and we've taken some steps to make that more possible. We renovated the first floor bathroom with accessible features, for example. And we could easily live here on one floor.

Land for Good helped us see our way to these conclusions. The consultants were very helpful in clearing our vision and guiding us to think this through.

Steve

In the process of exiting gradually, however, there's one thing that I simply couldn't endure. I couldn't stand to see the orchard fall into disrepair again. Couldn't stand to see it get overgrown and overtaken with apple scab and Plum Curculio. If there won't be someone to properly care for the orchard, I'd simply take the trees down. Put the orchard down, the way you'd put down a beloved old dog—lovingly and sorrowfully, but quietly and with respect.

For I am done with apple picking now
Robert Frost

RECIPES
from
Sentinel Farm

SO WE BECAME FARMERS

MEG'S APPLESAUCE

Like salt and pepper and paper napkins,
applesauce is a staple on our table at every meal

Apples*—enough to fill whatever large pot you choose to use.

Wash the apples well, then cut them into quarters. I usually cut off the blossom ends too, but that's optional.

Keep putting apples into the pot until it is full. Add 2-3 tablespoons of water or cider to keep the apples from sticking early in the process.

Bring the apples to a simmer, stirring and chopping occasionally, so they don't stick to the bottom of the pan. Cover the pan and look in occasionally, turning the apples and mashing them. Do this until all the apples are soft and mushy.

Put the cooked apples into a food mill such as a Foley or a chinois, and press until the sauce drips into a bowl, leaving behind the skins and seeds. Easy! Applesauce!

* I like to use Gravensteins because they yield a rosy sauce, but almost any variety of apple will do. Avoid McCoun because it's a hard apple and never seems to cook down acceptably.

CIDER JELLY

Apples are high in pectin and do the work of gelling

1 quart of apple cider

In a large saucepan (allow plenty of room for the syrup to bubble up), boil the apple cider to reduce it. When the cider has reduced to a syrup that coats a spoon, remove the pan from the heat and let the syrup cool. Don't overcook. The syrup will gel as it cools.

One quart of cider yields approximately 4 ounces of jelly.

MAPLE GRANOLA

3 cups uncooked, whole oatmeal (not instant)
1 cup raw almonds or pecans, coarsely chopped
1/4 cup extra virgin olive oil
1/4 cup Sentinel Farm maple syrup
1 teaspoon vanilla
1 cup golden raisins
sea salt, (optional)

Set the oven to 325 degrees. Line a large baking sheet with parchment. Combine all ingredients except the raisins and salt, and dump the mixture onto the parchment-covered baking sheet. With a potato masher, spread the granola evenly over the sheet and tamp it down firmly. Scatter the granola with a few pinches of sea salt, if desired. Bake for 45 minutes or until the granola is light brown. Cool. When cool, break up the granola and add the raisins. Store in a jar or plastic bag. For granola that is crisp and crunchy, store in the freezer.

STEVE'S BLUEBERRY PANCAKES

*Steve is the Sentinel Farm breakfast cook, He
whips these up whenever there is a houseful of guests*

1-1/2 cup flour
1 cup yellow stoneground cornmeal
2 teaspoons baking soda
1 teaspoon salt
2 tablespoons sugar
2 Sentinel Farm eggs, lightly beaten
2-1/2 cups buttermilk
1 stick of melted butter
    (alternatively, 6 tablespoons melted butter and 2
    tablespoons bacon drippings)
1-2 cups Sentinel Farm blueberries

Whisk together the flour, cornmeal, soda, salt, sugar. In
another bowl, combine the eggs, buttermilk and 6
tablespoons melted butter. Gently fold in the blueberries.

Heat a griddle to 350 degrees and coat it lightly with
melted butter or bacon drippings.

Pour the batter onto the griddle in circles of desired size.
When bubbles rise on side one, the pancakes are ready to
turn and cook on the other second side.

Serve with Sentinel Farm maple syrup.

Or, you can just use a couple boxes of Jiffy Cornmeal Mix

MAPLE BACON BRUSSELS SPROUTS

*At Sentinel Farm, we're still harvesting Brussels sprouts
from the garden at Thanksgiving and often beyond that.
Even non-fans of Brussels sprouts become enthusiasts
after tasting this recipe.*

1 pound baby Brussels sprouts, trimmed
1/4 cup olive oil
3 T Sentinel Farm maple syrup
4 slices of bacon, cut into 1/2-inch pieces
1/2 teaspoon kosher salt
1/4 teaspoon freshly ground black pepper

Preheat the oven to 400 degrees. Place sprouts in a single
layer in a baking dish and drizzle with oil then with syrup
and toss. Sprinkle on salt, pepper and bacon. Roast until the
bacon is crispy and the sprouts are carmelized—about 45
minutes. Stir halfway through the roasting time.

ABBY'S APPLE CRISP

4 medium-tart cooking apples, sliced (about 4 cups)
3/4 cup packed brown sugar
1/2 cup all purpose flour
1/2 cup oatmeal, quick-cooking or old-fashioned
1/3 cup butter, softened
3/4 teaspoon cinnamon

Set the oven to 375 degrees. Put a little water in the bottom of a glass baking dish—about 1/4 cup. Arrange the apple slices on the bottom of the dish and sprinkle the cinnamon over them. In a bowl, combine the oats, butter, brown sugar and flour and spread the mixture over the apples. Bake for 35-40 minutes or until the top is bubbly and golden brown.

MAPLE CRÈME BRULEE

This recipe uses a range of Sentinel Farm products
Plan to make it the day before your plan to serve it

6 yolks from Sentinel Farm hens
1/2 cup pure Sentinel Farm maple syrup
2 cups light cream or Sentinel Farm goat's milk
1 cup heavy cream
1 teaspoon vanilla extract
6 tablespoons of dark brown sugar

Preheat the oven to 325 degrees. Bring about 4 cups of water to a boil and reserve.

Very lightly whisk the egg yolks and maple syrup together. Set aside. In a heavy saucepan, scald the milk and cream together.

Gradually stir the hot cream into the yolks/maple syrup mixture until blended. Do not beat it or the finished texture will be grainy. Stir in the vanilla. Ladle mixture into six individual, oven-proof custard cups or ramekins of about 3/4-cup capacity, filling to the rim.

Place the cups in a large, shallow baking dish, then carefully pour in the boiled water until it reaches about halfway up the sides of the cups. Take care not to splash water into the cups.

Cover loosely with foil and bake for 1 hour until a knife inserted near the center comes out clean. Cool to room temperature, cover with plastic film, and refrigerate overnight.

About an hour before serving, remove the cups from the refrigerator. Sieve 1 tablespoon of brown sugar directly on the top of each custard, spreading it evenly with a fork. Put the cups in a shallow casserole, then pour in enough ice water to come halfway up the sides of the cups. Turn on the broiler and broil the custard close to the heat, until the brown sugar bubbles and darkens. Watch carefully or it will burn. Cool and serve.

MAPLE TRUFFLES

Peanut butter supplies protein;
maple syrup and cocoa are antioxidant superheroes
and provide calcium and magnesium as well.

1 cup all-natural crunchy peanut butter
1/2 cup Dutch process cocoa
1/2 cup Sentinel Farm maple syrup
***
Flaked coconut or ground nuts for rolling

In a large bowl, combine the peanut butter, cocoa and maple syrup. Refrigerate until the mixture can be molded by hand (Half to one hour). Shape the mixture into desired, truffle-sized balls and roll them in coconut or nuts. If the truffles are too cool to accept the coating, let them stand at room temperature until the coating sticks. Refrigerate the finished truffles.

GOAT'S MILK KEFIR

Kefir is a cultured, fermented beverage that tastes something like yogurt. Loaded with probiotic health, it uses "starter" grains that are a combination of yeasts, milk proteins and bacteria

Kefir grains*
1 quart goat's milk

In a quart-size mason jar, place one tablespoon of kefir grains. Pour one quart of goat's milk over the grains. Cover the jar with a cheesecloth or breathable towel and secure the towel with a rubber band. After 24 hours, stir the kefir. It will be thick.

*Kefir grains are available from health food stores and online sources such as Amazon.

MAGGIE'S HONEY COUGH ELIXIR

*This works on those annoying nighttime coughing spells that
sometimes come at the end of a bad cold*

1/4 cup Sentinel Farm honey
2-3 tablespoons strong Scotch whiskey

Mix the honey and whiskey in a small drinking glass and
leave the teaspoon in the glass. To quiet the coughing
spasm, take a teaspoon or more of the elixir and swallow
slowly, letting the honey coat the throat.

Maggie recommended avoiding the elixir after 4:00AM lest
you smell suspiciously alcoholic when you go to work.

GOAT MILK SOAP

12 ounces organic, unrefined coconut oil
15 ounces oil
13 ounces other oil (e.g. lard, sustainably-sourced palm oil,
tallow, vegetable shortening or other comparable oil)
13 ounces goat's milk, frozen
6 ounces lye (also called 100% sodium hydroxide, available
at local hardware stores
1 ounce essential oils, optional
Additives such as oatmeal or lavender flowers, optional

Mix the oils. Add the frozen goat's milk, then the lye. The
lye will warm the milk and thaw it. Finally, add whatever
essential oils and other additives of choice. Using a
handheld blender, blend the mixture to the consistency of
pudding. Pour into molds of choice or pour it into blocks to
be cutter later to desired size. Allow the mixture to harden
and cure.

SO WE BECAME FARMERS

RESOURCES

Community Involved in Sustaining Agriculture. (CISA) www.buylocalfood.org. Listings of local farms, farm stands and markets.

New England Vegetable & Fruit Conference (NEVF).

UMass Agricultural Extension and The Center for Agriculture, Food and the Environment (CARE). A wealth of information and programs of value to farmers. Contact: 413-545-4800. ag@cns.umass.edu.

Healthy Fruit UMass Extension, Fruit Program. Published weekly during the growing season from April to October. Most reports are from current research at UMass. Subscription cost is $65/year (electronic).

New England Tree Fruit Management Guide is published annually with contributors from Cornell University, UCONN, Univ. of Maine, UMass, Univ. of New Hampshire, Univ. of Vermont and the Univ. of Rhode Island.

UMass Fruit Advisor: umassfruit.com.

Scaffolds Fruit Journal: www.nysaes.cornell.edu/ent/scaffolds.

Massachusetts Maple Syrup Association

Maple Syrup Digest: Publication of the North American Maple Syrup Council and published four times a Year (Feb., June, Oct., Dec.).
www.northamericanmaple.org.
www.maple syrupdigest.org.

Land for Good. Landforgood.org. A 501©3 operation with the mission of ensuring the future of farming in New England by focusing on increasing farming opportunities, developing healthy lands and gaining a more secure food supply. Land for Good offers special programs for individuals interested in acquiring farms and farmland and for those interested in legacy programs and in transferring farms from one owner to the next. Offers a newsletter and programs to support farmers in all six New England states.

Harvest New England Association Inc. (HNE). A non-profit collaborative marketing program created in 1992 by New England state departments of agriculture with the mission of facilitating the sales of New England agricultural products through traditional and evolving marketing initiatives, brand stewardship, education, relationship building and support of research and policy development. HNE c/o Connecticut Department of Agriculture, Rm 127, 165 Capitol Ave., Hartford, CT 06106.

To read some of the research on the benefits of pure maple syrup, go to the University of Rhode Island website uri.org and search on maple syrup.

New England Vegetable & Berry Growers Assoc. (NEV&BGA). P.O. Box 882, Essex MA 01929.

Fiasco Farm for goat products and animal advice. fiascofarm.com.

SO WE BECAME FARMERS

DISCLAIMER

This is a memoir. The places, people, dates and events are as we remember them. If you remember things differently, well, that is your prerogative. And if you feel the record should be set straight you can always write your own memoir.

Meg and Steve

Additional copies of *SO WE BECAME FAMERS* are
available through
www.lulu.com
www.cheshirepress.com

You are welcome to visit Sentinel Farm
on Facebook or on the website: www.sentinelfarm.com

SO WE BECAME FARMERS